Contents

Teaching

Speaking & Listening

in the Primary School

Second Edition

Elizabeth Grugeon,
Lorraine Hubbard,
Carol Smith and Lyn Dawes

David Fulton Publishers
London

David Fulton Publishers Ltd
The Chiswick Centre, 414 Chiswick High Road, London W4 5TF

www.fultonpublishers.co.uk

First published in Great Britain by David Fulton Publishers 1998
Reprinted 1999, 2000, 2002
Second edition 2001

Note: The rights of the authors to be identified as the authors of this work has been asserted by them in accordance with the Copyright, Designs and Patents Act 1988.

Copyright © Elizabeth Grugeon, Lorraine Hubbard, Carol Smith and Lyn Dawes 2001

British Library Cataloguing in Publication Data
A catalogue record for this book is available from the British Library.

ISBN 1–85346–785–5

Typeset by FiSH Books, London
Printed and bound in Great Britain by Ashford Colour Press Limited, Gosport, Hants.

Acknowledgements

The authors would like to thank students and colleagues with whom they have worked at De Montfort University, Bedford for providing examples of their own and children's work. In particular, they would like to thank the children, staff and parents of Portfields Middle School, Newport Pagnell, Milton Keynes. Also the staff and children at Southway and The Cherry Trees Nursery Schools in Bedford.

The *Spoken Language and New Technology* (SLANT) project was a joint venture of the University of East Anglia and the Open University, funded 1990–93 by the Economic and Social Research Council (ESRC) (ref. R000232731). The *Talk, Reasoning and Computers* (TRAC) project is an Open University research project, also funded by the ESRC (ref. R000221868). This support, and the cooperation of teachers and children in schools in Buckinghamshire, Cambridgeshire, Milton Keynes, Northamptonshire and Norfolk, is gratefully acknowledged.

With thanks to Rosemary Smith, Lynda Gentle, Vyveanne Francis, Year 4 Primary BEd, De Montfort University, Bedford for their contribution to the Epilogue, and to Karen Martin for her contribution to Chapter 2.

In case of failure to obtain permission to include copyright material in this book the authors and publishers apologise and undertake to make good any omissions in subsequent printings.

Contributors

Lyn Dawes has been a primary science coordinator at a school in Milton Keynes and a teacher-researcher for the Open University. She has published widely in the field of speaking and listening in the primary school. Lyn has been involved with initial teacher education at De Montfort University and is currently Education Officer for the British Educational Communications and Technology Agency (BECTA).

Elizabeth Grugeon is Senior Lecturer in English in Primary Education at De Montford University, Bedford. She has led a research team, *Children Learning through Language*, and has teaching commitments in all areas of English teaching and a special interest in children's literature and children's oral culture. She is co-author (with Paul Gardner) of *The Art of Storytelling for Teachers and Pupils* (David Fulton Publishers).

Lorraine Hubbard was a primary school teacher in London and Devon. She was a researcher on the *Plymouth Early Years Language Project*. She is Senior Lecturer in English in Primary Education with an interest in literacy in the European context.

Carol Smith has been a primary teacher and English coordinator for many years. She is currently a literacy consultant working for Milton Keynes Learning and Development Directorate. Carol is also a visiting lecturer at the University of Hertfordshire and De Montfort University.

Introduction

What is Speaking and Listening all about?

Talk is a wonderful ready-made resource that each child brings to the first day of school – unlike the resources for reading and writing that the school provides. The danger is that we take talk for granted; we don't think we have to do anything. This book aims to give talk a voice, to highlight it and give it the attention it deserves. For at the heart of literacy is oracy, and the way we access literacy is through oracy. Teachers and researchers are developing ways to assess speaking and listening, to find out how children are learning and to structure opportunities for language development. Recent government initiatives have had an impact on the way we understand and approach the teaching of speaking and listening. These will be constantly referred to throughout this book.

Curriculum guidance for the foundation stage (Department for Education and Employment (DfEE)/Qualifications and Curriculum Authority (QCA) 2000: 44–5) puts the development and use of communication and language at the heart of young children's learning. The *National Literacy Strategy. Framework for Teaching* (DfEE 1998c: 3) puts speaking and listening at the centre of its definition of literacy:

> Literacy unites the important skills of reading and writing. It also involves speaking and listening which although they are not separately identified in the framework, are an essential part of it. Good oral work enhances pupils' understanding of language in both oral and written forms and of the way language can be used to communicate.

The National Literacy Strategy (NLS) framework and the introduction of the Literacy Hour have reinforced the importance of speaking and listening in the way the hour is delivered. The whole-class teaching component of the Literacy Hour requires a highly interactive, pacy oral exchange during which children need to pay close attention to the teacher and respond rapidly. Guided reading and writing sessions are also dependent on oral exchange between teacher and children while the independent group sessions require children to work in small self-motivated, collaborative discussion groups.

The *National Curriculum* (DfEE/QCA 1999), in which Speaking and Listening represents a third of the Programmes of Study for English, has introduced both 'Group discussion and interaction' and 'drama' under the heading 'Knowledge, Skills and Understanding', thus underpinning the more detailed prescription of the NLS.

For trainee teachers, the document, *Circular Number 4/98. Teaching: High Status, High Standards. Requirements for Courses of Initial Teacher Training* (DfEE 1998b), which lays down the statutory requirements for courses of initial teacher training (ITT) and specifies subject knowledge that teachers need at their own level in order to deliver the National Curriculum and NLS, is being revised. The revised version (2002) will have a significant emphasis on the role of Speaking and Listening. Providing a new definition of text that will include oral texts, it will recommend teaching strategies that promote interactive whole-class work and small group discussion, and the use of drama and role play to support the teaching of English.

However, despite more explicit support for speaking and listening, it is still the case that there is more detailed advice and support relating to the teaching of reading and writing. Speaking and Listening has tended to be an aspect of the English curriculum that is less rigorously and systematically planned, taught and assessed (Howe 1997: 1); it is an area in which many teachers feel that they need support and guidance. Teachers in training often feel this too.

A group of Primary BEd trainees, shortly before the implementation of the NLS in 1998, were discussing Speaking and Listening in the National Curriculum. A latecomer arrived and the lecturer casually asked her, 'What do you think about Speaking and Listening?' 'I think it should come first in everything we do!' she replied. And the talk moved on to consider how we can make that possible. How we can create opportunities for talk that address the requirements of the Programmes of Study for English; the 'Knowledge, Skills and Understanding' and 'Breadth of Study'. How we can plan for Speaking and Listening across the curriculum. And how examples of good practice can be drawn from school experience. The students discussed their experiences in a range of schools.

In sharing their experiences it became evident that Speaking and Listening is hard to identify. Although it represents one-third of the statutory requirement for English, this does not always seem to be reflected in the amount of time that is spent on it, the amount of planning dedicated to it and the evidence of assessment taking place. One student observed that, 'Speaking and Listening seems to be limited to responses to questions and being quiet when the teacher is talking'. Another's impressions were very different: 'I am in a Reception class where Speaking and Listening is given a high profile'. This was achieved in many ways, 'in formal settings where children are expected to observe the pragmatics of turn-taking, answering only when asked to do so, in informal settings where children are observed speaking with each other and the teacher and other adults interact with the children'. In this classroom, Pauline observed children telling stories, being involved in sharing nursery and number rhymes, and all taking part in the Christmas production. She also noticed how children were being encouraged to talk about their activities and observed the teacher's careful way of giving all children a chance to talk and to develop their confidence as speakers.

Students in lower primary classrooms had seen many examples of this kind which they felt had provided useful models for their own planning and which had extended their understanding of Speaking and Listening: 'I've seen some really interesting teaching of Speaking and Listening when children listened attentively and asked sensible and sensitive questions'. This was on an occasion when visitors had come into the classroom during a project entitled 'Young and Old'. Students were also becoming aware of the cross-curricular nature of talk and of group work, and the importance of pupils being able to take control of their own learning, 'You can see how vitally important children's group discussions are, they appreciate the chance to be in control'. Others felt that their experience of Speaking and Listening had been fairly limited during their school experiences and had not been aware of strategies being used either to promote or to assess Speaking and Listening: 'I have not seen any activity which a teacher has used to assess or develop these skills'.

This tendency was more pronounced for those students working with older primary classes: 'In my experience, Speaking and Listening has a very low status in teachers' planning. When I have tried to get children to discuss work in groups they have found this difficult. They don't see it as "sharing" ideas but as "copying". They feel more comfortable working individually so that the teacher gives each of them credit for their own thoughts'. Bernadine also wondered whether 'children have to be taught that although everybody has a different view, everybody's opinion is valid'. Caroline agreed that this was probably the case and raised another issue: that Speaking and Listening gives all children an opportunity to express their thoughts and opinions: 'I have witnessed discussion sessions in classrooms involving children confidently proposing ideas and opinions who would be unable to express themselves so well on paper'.

Several students were aware of potential problems, however. Di described how, 'during circle time, following a video or just during discussions in lessons, they are all very keen on speaking and getting over their ideas, experiences and viewpoints but not nearly so keen on listening to each other'. Again the seemingly low status of talk is mentioned. Kim observed that, 'apart from speaking as part of presentations, class assembly, Christmas performance etc. all other speaking seems to be little regarded. Children are rarely encouraged to discuss with one another, to argue a case against one another or to justify. They are allowed a little pointless chatter, are required to answer questions when asked and occasionally have to explain why something is the case. Other than these uses, speaking is generally discouraged'.

This would be unlikely to be the case today since all teachers will be planning from the NLS framework of objectives. However, at the time, others agreed that this was often their experience and as a consequence they felt less confident about planning for Speaking and Listening than they did for Reading and Writing: Anna admitted, 'I must confess that I am guilty of overlooking the importance of Speaking and Listening when planning my lessons and do not feel that I am a confident teacher of Speaking and Listening'. Many in this group felt like Anna. Kim raised other general concerns: 'Apart from being unsure about control issues, I would like to encourage more Speaking and Listening and be able to teach such skills but I would be insecure about assessing these skills'.

Many students in training and newly qualified teachers may empathise with Kim in feeling that teaching Speaking and Listening could involve considerable risks. In the past, priorities in ITT have tended to squeeze the amount of time devoted to the subject. This is not likely to be the case in future; the English Orders (DfEE/QCA1999), the many NLS initiatives relating to Speaking and Listening during 2002, and the introduction of the new Key Stage 3 National Literacy Study Framework, where Speaking and Listening is a major strand, will all support a more confident approach by trainees and teachers. This book will provide a rationale for the centrality of Speaking and Listening in English and across the curriculum, based on evidence of good practice. It will provide an argument for developing talk in the classroom that gives Speaking and Listening equal status with Reading and Writing in the acquisition of literacy.

Speaking and Listening issues: a review

Teachers may well feel that everything in education has been undergoing major changes, not least as far as the teaching of English is concerned. The implementation of the NLS has been the focus of much attention and concern for standards of literacy will continue to affect children as they enter school, and new teachers as they enter the profession. *The National Literacy Strategy. Framework for Teaching* (DfEE 1998c) was introduced to raise standards in literacy. It was accompanied by a government target, 'By 2002 80% of 11 year olds should reach the standard expected for their age in English (i.e. Level 4) in the Key Stage 2 National Curriculum tests' (DfEE 1998b: 5). The new strategy was introduced in order to achieve this target, and it involved both the training of primary teachers and the professional development of serving primary teachers. For students in training the highest priority was to be given to ensuring that they were taught 'in accordance with nationally established criteria – how to teach literacy' (Literacy Task Force 1997: 22). The DfEE subsequently provided these criteria in *Requirements for Courses of Initial Teacher Training. Circular 4/98* (DfEE 1998a) followed by *Circular 4/98, Teaching: High Status, High Standards. Requirements for Courses of Initial Teacher Training* (DfEE 1998b) which is being revised and will be reissued in 2002.

The ITT National Curriculum for primary English sent an, 'unequivocal message about the importance of literacy by specifying the essential core of knowledge, understanding and skills which all primary trainees . . . must be taught' (DfEE 1998b: 20). *The National Literacy Strategy. Framework for Teaching* (DfEE 1998c) was accompanied by in-service education and training (INSET) for teachers in schools. Teachers, and teachers in training, have had to take on board a new focus on standards as far as their own knowledge and understanding are concerned (DfEE 1998a). Trainees have become accustomed to keeping a detailed record of their knowledge and understanding in relation to the standards required by Circular 4/98.

For children entering compulsory education a national framework for baseline assessment has become a statutory requirement. *Curriculum guidance for the foundation stage* (DfEE/QCA 2000) describes 'stepping stones' towards the Early Learning Goals, which most children should achieve by the end of Reception, the foundation stage. The foundation stage curriculum is organised into six areas of learning, one of which is 'communication, language and literacy'. And here we find that, 'the development and use of communication and language is at the heart of young children's learning'. The revised National Curriculum for English (DfEE/QCA 1999) builds on this; the central importance of Speaking and Listening as the means of teaching and learning both Reading and Writing is reaffirmed. However, while the NLS does not make the teaching of Speaking and Listening explicit in the framework, it is implicit at all times. In the revised National Curriculum, the Programme of Study for Speaking and Listening at Key Stages 1 and 2 (DfEE/QCA 1999) extends 'skills' to include 'group discussion and interaction' and also 'drama activities'; under 'range of purposes' are specific suggestions as to what should be included such as, 'investigating, selecting, sorting, planning, predicting, exploring, explaining, reporting, evaluating' (DfEE/QCA 1999: 24). These skills underpin the requirements of the NLS and reinforce the centrality of Speaking and Listening.

The revised Programmes of Study for all National Curriculum subjects emphasise the importance of the interrelationship of Speaking and Listening, Reading and Writing in the provision of an integrated curriculum. The new orders stress these links: English contributes to the school curriculum by developing pupils' abilities to speak, listen, read and write for a wide range of purposes, using language to communicate ideas, views and feelings (DfEE/QCA 1999: 2).

The main aim of this book, therefore, is to provide evidence of the value of Speaking and Listening and to support this by reference to classroom strategies that involve an integrated approach to literacy. But teachers still want to consider what may be lost if the subject, English, is redefined as 'literacy'. There is a continuing need to demonstrate the centrality of Speaking and Listening to any definition of literacy.

Each chapter is self-contained, looking at different aspects of Speaking and Listening in the primary school. Chapter 1 provides an introduction to issues and the context for subsequent discussion, Chapter 2 looks at a range of practical concerns for early years' teachers. Chapter 3 combines practice and theory in storytelling and narrative in the early years. Chapter 4 discusses the way teachers achieve continuity and progression at Key Stage 2. Chapter 5 focuses on work with older children, exploring the teaching of 'ground rules' for talk in small group collaborative activity. Chapter 6 links issues for Key Stages 1 and 2 in an overview of different approaches to assessment.

CHAPTER 1

Speaking and Listening: An Overview

Prologue

As teachers we all have special moments of insight, 'epiphanies', when something we had never thought of or noticed before becomes crystal clear and nothing is ever the same again. Years ago, I was a part-time tutor on an Open University education course called *Language and Learning*. One of the assignments I had to mark was part of a study unit called *Language in the Classroom*, written by Douglas Barnes (1973). At the time, in 1973, this unit broke new ground by asking teachers to focus on the idea of 'classroom communication', of 'the classroom as a context for language' and of 'talking in order to learn'; these were new and challenging ideas for many teachers. Although teachers of English in both primary and secondary schools, at that time, were likely to feel comfortable about promoting interactive talk in the classroom, teachers in other curriculum areas tended to give small group collaborative talk a fairly low priority. Indeed, pupil talk was more likely to be in response to teacher questioning than initiated by the pupils; the amount of pupil talk in the classroom was very much related to issues of control and discipline.

The Open University assignment required the students taking this course – all of whom were practising teachers – to make a recording of a small group of children talking together as they undertook a particular task without a teacher being present. They had to transcribe the children's discussion and write an account of what seemed to be happening, looking for evidence of ways in which the children might be working together and helping each other to solve a problem or make sense of the situation they were dealing with.

You have to believe me when I say that this was a very novel idea at the time. Barnes had to give considerable encouragement to students doing the assignment:

> The longer you can spend working on the cassette tape and transcription the more you will understand about what is going on in it. It would be a mistake to dismiss speech as too obvious for close attention: the tape-recorder is making us aware of aspects of our behaviour which had previously hardly been guessed at. You will be making explicit to yourself perceptions which in everyday talk we experience intuitively, or perhaps not at all. Most of us have not learnt to be aware of how

speech operates, so that learning to perceive what is going on in quite an ordinary dialogue demands care and patience.   (1973: 21)

In asking his students to record children talking on their own, he writes:

> I want you to listen to a group of children talking when there is no teacher present to direct them. There are several reasons for beginning with children's uses of language when they are alone. Most importantly, it will allow you to see something of how children are able to adapt their language resources to cope with learning tasks.   (1973: 20)

One of the students in my tutorial group was a teacher in a small rural primary school and her transcript and comments were to make a major contribution to my own understanding. We want you to read it for yourselves. Try to identify how the children are adapting their language resources to cope with the learning task, before you move on to the second part when the teacher comes into the room. The transcript is in two parts. (It might help to read and discuss this with someone else.)

Transcript: Three children in a lower school, seven and six years-old, discuss snails in a snailery, without their teacher present

Susan:	Yes, look at this one, it's come ever so far. This one's stopped for a little rest ...
Jason:	It's going again!
Susan:	Mmmm ... good!
Emma:	This one's ... smoothing ... slowly
Jason:	Look, they've bumped into each other (laughter)
Emma:	It's sort of like got four antlers
Susan:	Where?
Emma:	Look! I can see their eyes
Susan:	Well, they're not exactly eyes ... they're a second load of feelers really ... aren't they? No ... and they grow bigger you know ... and at first you couldn't hardly see the feelers and then they start to grow bigger, look ...
Emma:	Look ... look at this one he's really come ... out ... now
Jason:	It's got water on it when they move
Susan:	Yes, they make a trail, no ... let him move and we see the trail afterwards ...
Emma:	I think it's oil from the skin ...
Jason:	Mmm ... it's probably ... moisture ... See, he's making a little trail where he's been ... they ... walk ... very ... slowly
Susan:	Yes, Jason, this one's doing the same, that's why they say slow as a snail
Emma:	Ooh look, see if it can move the pot ...
Jason:	Doesn't seem to

Susan:	Doesn't like it in the p ... when it moves in the pot ... look, get him out!
Jason:	Don't you dare pull its ... shell off
Emma:	You'll pull its thing off ... shell off ... ooh it's horrible!
Jason:	Oh look ... all this water!

At this point, the teacher came back and joined the discussion. It is worth considering what has been going on in this brief discussion before you read the second part. For example: how are the children interacting? How are they using language? Is there evidence of shared understanding?

Teacher:	Can you tell me how you think they move?
Emma:	Very slowly
Teacher:	Jason, you tell me, how are they moving?
Jason:	They're pushing theirselves along
Teacher:	How many feet can you see?
Susan:	Don't think they have got any feet, really
Teacher:	None at all?
Susan:	No
Emma:	I should say they've got ... can't see 'em, no
Susan:	Haven't exactly got any feet
Emma:	Slide ... the bottom ... so it slides ... they can go along
Teacher:	Doesn't it look like one big foot?
All:	Yes ... yes (*murmur hesitantly*)
Teacher:	Where do you think its eyes are?
Emma:	On those little bits
Susan:	I can see ... little
Teacher:	Which little bits?
Susan:	You see those little bits at the bottom
Teacher:	Yes? You think the top bits? Which ones do you think, Susan?
Susan:	I think the bottom one
Teacher:	You think the bottom ... well, have a close look at the bottom horns, what is the snail doing with the bottom horns?
Susan:	He is feeling along the ground
Teacher:	He's feeling along, so what would you call the bottom horns, Jason?
Susan:	Arms? No ... sort of ...
Emma:	Legs?
Teacher:	You think they're legs, you think they're arms. What do you think they are, Jason, if he's feeling with them?
Jason:	Feelers?

Reflections on this episode

You may have noticed the way the children responded to this task; their thoughtful and creative use of language to explore and define what they were observing, 'it's smoothing slowly', 'It's sort of got four antlers'; the way they were working as a group, listening and responding to each other's contributions, 'I think it's oil', 'it's probably moisture'. When she listened to the recording, their teacher was surprised to discover what they were capable of observing and describing on their own and felt that she might have given them more chance to tell her what they had found out for themselves before she started on her own agenda. She was concerned by the way that she had asked closed questions that required a single word correct answer; an approach which did not encourage them to share speculations in the way they were doing when they were on their own. In Chapter 5 we look more closely at the way children work together in small discussion groups and consider whether this kind of 'cumulative' talk, where the speaker builds positively but uncritically on what the other has said, has its limitations. It is possible that when the teacher joins them they are beginning to need an adult presence; their investigative behaviour is beginning to alarm them, they are worried that they might harm the snails. The teacher, despite her misgivings, moves them on by helping them to use appropriate subject-specific language; Jason has learned the term 'feelers' by the end of the transcript.

It is a tribute to Douglas Barnes' pioneering work that we no longer find being asked to look closely at this sort of transcript surprising. At the time, my student and I were on a steep learning curve and I have never forgotten her amazement and the way she wrote movingly about the new insights that listening to her children working on their own had given her. She was surprised to discover what the children were capable of. She was delighted by the shared excitement and use of language to explore what was going on; describing, questioning, speculating, hypothesising and sharing ideas tentatively. She noted the way they used tag questions like, 'aren't they?' to include each other in the group, put forward their ideas tentatively, 'I think it's ... ' , 'it's probably', 'it's sort of ... ', 'well, they're not exactly ... ', 'it doesn't seem to ... '; she noticed how they first observed and then tried to find words to explain what they could see, 'stopped', 'going', 'smoothing', 'bumped' and then focused on detail, drawing each others' attention, 'look', 'see', as they set up an experiment, 'let him move and we see the trail afterwards', 'see if it can move the pot'. Then, as she continued to analyse the recording, she described how when she returned to the classroom, her questions had put an end to this reflective talk, how by imposing her agenda she had given them no chance to tell her what they already knew and what was interesting them. She commented on the way in which she had taken over and finally produced the answers that she wanted without realising that they had already used the word 'feelers' on their own and talked about how the snails moved. She commented on the fact that out of 27 utterances, she had contributed 11, all questions, and that Jason had made only two contributions, both answers. When she transcribed the recording of what the children were saying before she joined them, she admitted to feeling mortified! And I shared this feeling, knowing how often I had imposed my own agenda on a class without listening to them and finding out what the children already knew. For me, this small episode marked the beginning of my participation in a growing awareness among teachers of the centrality of talk to learning and of the need to listen to our pupils and to ourselves as teachers.

I still use this transcript with my education students as an introduction to sessions on talking and learning. A quarter of a century later, it continues to make a point about what children can do and already know and how important it is to listen to them.

Oracy: issues and concerns

You may be more familiar with the term 'literacy' than you are with 'oracy': it refers to Speaking and Listening and is spelt out in the Programmes of Study for English (DfEE/QCA 1999). At Key Stage 1: 'Pupils learn to speak clearly, thinking about the needs of their listeners. They work in small groups and as a class, joining in discussions and making relevant points. They also learn how to listen carefully to what other people are saying, so that they can remember the main points. They learn to use language in imaginative ways and express their ideas and feelings when working in role and in drama activities' (DfEE/QCA 1999: 16). And at Key Stage 2: 'Pupils learn how to speak in a range of contexts, adapting what they say and how they say it to the purpose and the audience. Taking varied roles in groups gives them opportunities to contribute to situations with different demands. They also learn to respond appropriately to others, thinking about what has been said and the language used' (DfEE/QCA 1999: 22).

These detailed requirements have implications for planning and organisation across the curriculum:

> Children's talk can no longer be . . . seen simply as a means to an end. We need to be much more aware of the learning potential of talk; of the ways in which teaching might assist children's spoken language development; of the best ways of gathering information and eventually making informed assessments of children's talk; and through all of this, how our behaviour as teachers in our planning of the curriculum, in our interactions with children and our discussions with other colleagues, can best contribute to the kind of classroom and school climate most conducive to oracy.
>
> (Howe 1997: 2)

In this book we shall explore some of these issues; discussing the learning potential of talk, considering how our planning can assist the development of children's spoken language and how we can describe and assess this development. Since the publication of *Use of Language: A Common Approach* (School Curriculum and Assessment Authority (SCAA) 1997c), which considered ways in which language and learning might be developed across the curriculum, the NLS has introduced practical approaches to raising standards in the classroom. It has become evident that speaking and listening skills underpin developments in literacy; that teaching and learning depend upon them. This fact is acknowledged in all curriculum areas in the National Curriculum (DfEE/QCA 1999) but as there is no statutory testing of speaking and listening, its status in relation to reading and writing has been less certain. Schools and teachers are less sure about how to measure progress in talk or how to develop strategies for assessment that mirror their assessment of the more permanent and observable skills of reading and writing. Office for Standards in Education (OFSTED) inspectors have also been aware that speaking and listening was not being inspected as effectively as reading and writing. It seemed that inspectors shared teachers' uncertainty about the assessment of speaking and listening (see National Association for the Teaching of English (NATE) 1996). What counts as evidence of good performance and how we can develop more reliable strategies for assessment will be topics of concern in this book. It might help to begin by looking at the reasons for this uncertainty and why the need for description, analysis and assessment of speaking and listening have taken time to emerge and why what has been described as the 'richest resource' for teachers (Norman 1992: 2) can still prove problematic.

The emergence of oracy

At the start of the 1990s, a national project was under way – schools in a number of local authorities had become involved in a practical exploration of the role of talk in the classroom. Oracy was the buzzword. At nursery, primary and secondary levels, teachers, working with local and national coordinators, were embarking on uncharted territory – to create a classroom-based theory of learning centred on talk. The National Oracy Project (NOP) was to break new ground: it established new understanding and made a major contribution to the structure of English in the National Curriculum where, for the first time, Speaking and Listening was to be given equal status to Reading and Writing as attainment targets.

The National Oracy Project 1987–93

This was set up by the School Curriculum Development Committee and was administered by the National Curriculum Council (NCC). It was a curriculum development project based on action research by teachers in their classrooms. The aims of the project were to

- enhance the role of speech in the learning process 5–16 by encouraging active learning;
- develop the teaching of oral communication skills;
- develop methods of assessment of and through speech, including assessment for public examinations at 16+;

- improve pupils' performance across the curriculum;
- enhance teachers' skills and practice;
- promote recognition of the value of oral work in schools and increase its use as a means of improving learning (Norman 1992: xii).

The NOP was the natural successor to the highly successful National Writing Project (1985–88) which has had a profound effect on the understanding and practice of the teaching of writing. The Oracy Project was, however, to a large extent tackling a new aspect of learning: the importance of talk had been gradually emerging as fundamental to children's learning. It was often acknowledged implicitly but rarely made explicit in planning for the majority of curriculum subjects. The project had a powerful influence on the content and focus of the National Curriculum requirements for Speaking and Listening.

Early research 1965–76: a focus on talking and learning

The term oracy, as opposed to literacy and numeracy, emerged in the 1960s. It was coined by Andrew Wilkinson who was researching classroom talk at Birmingham University. His project was to provide early evidence of the way individuals learn through talk and particularly by working cooperatively in small groups (Wilkinson *et al.* 1965). Research carried out by Douglas Barnes in Leeds and by Harold Rosen and the London Association for the Teaching of English continued to identify classroom conditions that seemed to lead to successful learning. This led to the publication of two influential texts, *Language, the Learner and the School* (Barnes *et al.* 1969) and *From Communication to Curriculum* (Barnes 1976).

The growing evidence that pupils' learning might be enhanced by working collaboratively in small groups encouraged teachers to begin to question their reliance on a transmission model of teaching, in which they took control of what was to be learned and did most of the speaking while pupils listened. The focus shifted to considering ways of also allowing pupils to use their own language to formulate their own questions, to speculate and hypothesise about the topics and material that they were being taught. The idea that pupils might take a more active role in making sense of the curriculum began to take root. However, despite much attention to oral language and a number of research projects suggesting a variety of initiatives – in particular the use of small group work – these were slow to be taken up in schools.

The Bullock Committee's enquiry into the teaching of English, *A Language for Life* (Department of Education and Science (DES) 1975), endorsed the use of oral language and small group teaching strategies and stressed that schools should recognise that language was a cross-curricular responsibility.

We welcome the growth in interest in oral language in recent years, for we cannot emphasise too strongly our conviction of its importance in the education of the child . . . But there is still a great deal to be done. A priority objective for all schools

is a commitment to the speech needs of their pupils and a serious study of the role
of oral language in learning.   (DES 1975: 10.30)

However, as Keiner explained, in a succinct history of the NOP, the time was not right:

> Unfortunately, the report was published at a time when Britain was facing its
> gravest financial crisis since World War Two. No funds were available to support
> the recommendations of the report ... different agendas were appearing during the
> 1970s, with more fundamental questioning of the education system itself.
>
> (Keiner 1992)

A series of Her Majesty's Inspectorate (HMI) reports throughout the 1970s and early
1980s gives evidence that little attention was being paid to the development of
speaking and listening. However, HMI was encouraging enthusiastic teachers to
develop oral work in the classroom and by 1982 the government was giving explicit
priority to curriculum development in oracy; in 1986 funding became available and
plans for the NOP were finalised. At the same time, proposals to establish a National
Curriculum set in motion a programme of educational reform. 'The curriculum for
English was to bring speaking and listening onto the statutory agenda for every
classroom' (Keiner 1992: 253). This proved to be problematic. Models of good practice
and assessment were few and far between; the NOP was going to have to provide
answers almost before it had begun to articulate the questions.

> Those who had worked for so long to establish a NOP could scarcely have imagined
> that, within months of its launch, the profession would look to it to provide rapid
> answers to fundamental questions about the implementation and assessment of what
> had suddenly become a statutory classroom requirement.
>
> (Keiner 1992: 254)

The inheritance of the NOP: a statutory classroom requirement

All this may seem like water under the bridge but it is important not to underestimate
the value of the early work of Douglas Barnes, Andrew Wilkinson and Harold Rosen
that had put spoken language at the centre of children's learning. The emphasis may
have shifted slightly from 'talking' to 'speaking', as a concern for language skills and
standard English have entered the literacy debate, but the interdependence of the three
language modes is now taken for granted: speaking and listening is acknowledged as
an integral part of learning to read and write and central to the development of literacy.

The pioneering work of the NOP teachers and coordinators in the early 1990s laid
the foundations for the implementation of the Speaking and Listening requirements of
the English National Curriculum and established benchmarks for practice and
assessment. Its publications have provided the practical and theoretical underpinning
for classrooms, teacher training and further research.

The revised National Curriculum Programmes of Study for English (DfEE/QCA1999) as we have seen, pay considerable attention to the importance of group discussion and interaction. This new emphasis is a response to the structure of the Literacy Hour which requires pupils to work independently in small groups. They will need new skills if they are going to be able to 'talk effectively as members of a group' (DfEE/QCA 1999: 22). These skills will often need specific teaching (see Chapter 5).

Group discussion and interaction: exploratory talk

To illustrate some of the basic principles in curriculum work in oracy that were established by the NOP, we would like you to start by looking at a transcript of a group of 11-year-olds who are discussing a poem on their own. Before you read the transcript you might like to read the short poem and discuss it with a friend. It will be interesting to compare the way you thought about it with the way the boys responded. If you are able to collaborate with others it may help you to think about the value of talk in your own learning and understanding.

Looking at an example of small group talk

The transcript is a recording of four Year 6 boys who have been asked to discuss a poem, *The Small Dust-Coloured Beetle* by Robert Bloomfield. It is an eighteenth-century poem and some of the language may seem slightly obscure. See what you make of it before you discuss the boys' response.

The Small Dust-Coloured Beetle

The small dust-coloured beetle climbs with pain
O'er the smooth plantain leaf, a spacious plain!
Thence higher still, by countless steps convey'd
He gains the summit of a shivering blade,
And flirts his filmy wings, and looks around,
Exulting in his distance from the ground.

Activity

You will need about an hour to complete this activity:

- Read the poem and talk about it with colleagues. If possible, record your discussion. The boys were asked to talk about the poem and anything that it made them think about.
- Read the extract from the boys' discussion – bearing in mind that they continued to discuss this poem at greater length. Long stretches of transcript can seem daunting so read this one through to get an impression of the general strategies that are being used.

- Choose a shorter extract – say five utterances – for more detailed analysis. Looking at very small stretches of transcript in some detail can give you an insight into the way group interaction and sharing talk may enable individual discovery to take place. The following questions may help you to do this.

1. In what ways do the members of this group
    (a) support each others' contribution?
    (b) extend each others' contribution?
    (c) modify each others' contribution?
2. What is the role of the poem in this discussion?
    (a) Does it constrain or open up possibilities for discussion?
    (b) Would it have been the same sort of discussion if they had been observing a live beetle? If not, how does the fact that they are talking about a poem affect the discussion?
3. Where and how do you feel that you can see
    (a) problem solving taking place?
    (b) shared learning taking place?

Transcript: Extract from a discussion of a poem

Mark:	How does she know it's in pain? When it, where it says, 'the small dust-coloured beetle climbs with pain'. Does she know it's in pain?
Kenneth:	Ah – come on Simmy, if something's small, really, er climbing, something small to us, is very big to him, it must be tired, you've got to allow that you're going to be tired, ain't yer?
John:	Yeah, you can see what it means this poem, because it would be hard for a beetle to climb up a leaf, wouldn't it?
Mark:	It must be breathless, because the, I mean, you know, it's kind of going...
John:	Mmm
Mark:	A leaf, if it is a leaf, isn't, er, very big though, compared with a beetle
John:	No, that's true, it depends what kind of beetle it is ...
Kenneth:	'Spacious plain'
John:	No – it says 'spacious plain' so it must be quite big ...
Kenneth:	It is big to a beetle ...
Clive:	I think the beetle must be small because not many leaves ...
John:	Because there's lots of different kinds of beetles and it's probably small
Clive:	Unless it's a dock leaf, that can be pretty big
John:	or rhubarb ...
Mark:	That must really, that must be hard work for a little beetle, mustn't it? 'specially that colour
Kenneth:	It is
Clive:	And beetles' legs aren't exactly the biggest

John:	Not very long
Kenneth:	Ah look, they are not very thick to us but surely they're quite thick to a beetle
John:	Yeah, you see, because if you look at, say if a beetle's ...
Mark:	They'd think this is a leaf, they could easily just fly on to it ... couldn't they?
John:	Yeah, it all depends whether they're winged beetles or not
Kenneth:	Yeah, why would it climb if it could fly to the top?
John:	Yeah, so it must be, it can't really be able to fly, can it?
Mark:	It must be, because look, um, 'flirts his filmy wings'
Kenneth:	Yeah, but some of these have small sort of wings, but don't fly
John:	Yeah, you look at an ostrich or a penguin
Mark:	I wonder what kind of beetle this is ... it could be a ladybird, it could be any kind of beetle for all we know
John:	But there again, it could be a weak little thing that could fly down but not up
John:	Yeah, perhaps it has to have a high point to start off flying, you know, so it doesn't fall, it can't take off ...
Mark:	Has to have a wind
John:	I doubt if it could fly against wind
Kenneth:	It says 'a small dust-coloured beetle'
John:	It's probably a wood beetle
Clive:	Woodlouse
John:	Yeah, woodlouse, that's right ... and another thing that proves it's big it says, um ...
Mark:	'By countless steps'
John:	'Thence higher still, by countless steps convey'd'
Kenneth:	And 'exulting in his distance from the ground'
John:	So, not only must the leaf be big, but the plant he's on must be quite ...

Comment

You may have talked in general about the determined way that the four boys keep on task, the way that they are listening to each other, their attention to detail, their concern to establish what kind of beetle it is. They could as easily be examining a specimen under a microscope but here they are scrutinising a poem where the words offer them the clues and evidence they need.

Answering the questions above, you may have noticed:

1. (a) the way they express support for each other's ideas: *mmm ... yeah ... you can see what it means*
   (b) the way they extend each other's comments: Mark: *How does she know it's in pain?* Kenneth: *it must be tired,* John: *it would be hard,* Mark: *it must be breathless*

(c) the way they modify each other's contributions: John modifies Mark's comment, *they could easily just fly on to it . . . couldn't they?* with, *it all depends whether they're winged beetles or not.*

Looking more closely at the interaction you may have identified some of the tentative ways they try out ideas and speculate. In the first five utterances, for example, you may have identified examples of the way they:

ask questions: *does she know it's in pain?*
speculate and hypothesise: *if something's small . . . it must be tired*
reason: *because it would be hard . . .*
give evidence: *it must be breathless because*
make assertions: *it must be tired . . . you've got to allow that*
use tags to signal tentativeness: *wouldn't it?*
tolerate each other's efforts to express an idea: *because the, I mean, you know . . .*

2. The fact that they are discussing a poem rather than observing a live beetle seems to focus their attention on the meaning of the words. They use these to support their hypothesis about the size of the beetle. Notice the way Mark, John and Kenneth quote from the text in the last four lines of the extract but at the same time draw on their experience and knowledge about insects and plants.
3. (a) and (b) You probably identified examples of problem solving and found evidence of learning taking place as they discussed the probable size of the beetle or whether it could fly, *perhaps it has to have a high point, has to have a wind, I doubt if it could fly against wind . . .*

Pupil talk and learning

Teachers working together during the NOP spent much time recording and analysing their pupils' speaking and listening. One of the conclusions that they reached was that all pupils need opportunities to work together in small groups, 'making meaning through talk, supported by their peers' (Des-Fountain and Howe 1992: 146). They drew up a set of general principles about the value of pupil–pupil talk which were based on their examination of their pupils working together. They used Barnes' theoretical exploration of the role of talk in learning to bridge the gap between theory and practice. Their principles, based on classroom evidence, support assertions that in a classroom where pupils are engaged in shared social and interactive talk:

- a readiness to learn can be created;
- pupils can work on ideas together;
- opportunities can be created for pupils to make sense of new information;
- pupils working together can provide social support for the learning process;
- tentatively expressed thoughts can become clearer in well-structured group activities.

You might like to consider the value of pupil–pupil talk. The following questions could be the basis for drawing up your own list of principles.

- How might it help pupils to talk about a task before they tackle it?
- What are the advantages of working on ideas together?
- When does it help to have the teacher in the group?
- What difference might it make if the teacher is not in the group?

You may have considered some of the following ideas:

- Through talk, pupils can recall and review what they already know and define what more they want to know about a topic.
- If pupils have already contributed their own ideas they will have a greater stake in their learning.
- Pupils who are struggling with literacy can use talk to make sense of new information.
- Ideas can be tried out to see how they sound ('How do I know what I mean until I hear what I say?').
- 'Provisional' meanings can be made as the group negotiates shared understanding.
- Tentativeness can be valued and supported because pupils are more likely to say 'I don't understand'.
- Working in a supportive peer group will help pupils to learn in the variety of English or the community language which bests suits their needs.
- Pupils can provide each other with an authentic audience, giving an immediate and engaged response which values others' contributions.
- The peer group can tolerate the need for 'thinking time' (involving social talk and silence).
- Pupils are more likely to ask each other questions in order to make meaning clearer and expand and interpret each other's ideas.

(Based on Norman 1992: 144–5)

You might like to reflect on the extent to which you identified any of these principles when you were discussing the transcript of the boys talking about the poem *The Small Dust-Coloured Beetle*.

The central role of exploratory talk in cognitive development

Over the last ten years, research that grew from the activities of NOP has deepened our awareness of the power of group talk to extend intellectual development, and the ways that teachers can build this into the social context for learning in the classroom. In her book, *The Articulate Classroom*, Prue Goodwin (2001) warns us that the National Curriculum may be missing an important dimension: 'the programme of study for speaking and listening emphasises the development of social skills almost to the exclusion of the cognitive', and there is a 'lack of specific direction in the English Order concerning the central role of exploratory talk'. The exploratory nature of cognitive talk might be seen to be in conflict with the social demands of the National Curriculum as 'there is little recognition of the way learners work on their own understanding by talking through learning tasks' (Goodwin 2001: xii).

This concern for the cognitive aspect is reiterated in research summarised by Roy Corden (2000: 97):

> for successful group learning to occur, teachers need to consider the relationship between the social, communicative and cognitive aspects of talking and learning and to structure tasks carefully in terms of social interdependence and cognitive demand.

Neil Mercer (2000: 1) has coined the term 'interthinking' to connect the social and cognitive functions of group talk. He describes interthinking as 'our use of language for thinking together, for collectively making sense of experience and solving problems. We do this "interthinking" in ways which most of us take for granted but which are at the heart of human achievement'.

Collaborative talk and assessment

Returning to the National Curriculum, we can see how many of the principles that emerged from curriculum development and research have been translated into the revised National Curriculum (DfEE/QCA 1999). The Programmes of Study for English and other subjects emphasise the value of collaborative work and we need to ensure that we make space for this kind of oral work in our planning. The NOP left no doubt about the importance of Speaking and Listening across the curriculum and the value of close scrutiny of transcripts of group discussion both for diagnostic and assessment purposes.

Collecting and using evidence of talk

We are aware that there is little time for you to collect and analyse samples of pupils' talk. Pupils can be encouraged to record their own talk when working together in a group. Listening to, reflecting on and discussing their collaboration will give them the opportunity to assess their own work and to become articulate about the relationship between talk and learning. There are examples of the kinds of formats that you might use to do this in Chapter 6. Recording their own talk, in role play and drama could also provide material for discussing the key skills such as identifying and using standard English for appropriate purposes and audiences. Speaking and Listening is perhaps, the hardest of the Programmes of Study to identify and describe for assessment purposes. Writing and reading clearly permeate and underpin all curriculum subjects; it generates specific texts that can be controlled and accounted for. Speaking and listening is harder to categorise. At a general level, the National Curriculum identifies two broad areas to be taught and assessed across the English Programmes of Study: 'Knowledge, Skills and Understanding' and 'Breadth of Study'. The level descriptions for Speaking and Listening are rather generally described and assigning children to the appropriate level is hard to do with any degree of accuracy.

Assigning levels

We might try to decide which levels Mark, Kenneth, John and Clive have reached. At Level 2 children are required to be able to, 'listen carefully and respond with increasing appropriateness to what others say'. Presumably, we could safely say that from the evidence of the transcript all the boys have reached Level 2; but what else might we want to say about their performance? At Level 3, we are asked to identify whether they can, 'talk and listen confidently in different contexts'. Clearly the evidence of one transcript could not tell us whether that is the case and we would need to account for a variety of different activities over a period of time. We would also need evidence that individuals were, 'beginning to be aware of Standard English and when it is used'. Looking at the transcript, we might say that there is evidence of this, as only one non-standard form is used, ain't yer, and that in this informal group of friends the use of a dialect form is appropriate. The way that they quote from the poem, 'thence higher still, by countless steps convey'd' shows that they are confidently 'using a growing vocabulary' (Level 2). Using the level descriptions, we could say that as a group they have reached Level 4 (which would be appropriate for their age and stage).

> Level 4. Pupils talk and listen with confidence in an increasing range of contexts. Their talk is adapted to the purpose: developing ideas thoughtfully; describing events and conveying their opinions clearly. In discussion, they listen carefully, making contributions and asking questions that are responsive to others' ideas and views. They use appropriately some of the features of standard English vocabulary and grammar.
>
> (DfE 1995a)

We could confidently assign Level 4 to the group but we might feel less sure about which level to award to individual members of the group. It is through their interaction and collaboration as a group that the boys achieve Level 4 and perhaps, learn the skills that are required to achieve Level 4. The essentially interactive and social nature of speaking and listening makes assessment difficult. However, this kind of group discussion seems to enable the participants to experience working at a higher level than they might have been able to achieve on their own. (For a broader discussion of assessment of Speaking and Listening see Chapter 6.)

Knowledge, skills and understanding: standard English and language variation

The requirements at Key Stages 1 and 2 for quite specific language study in relation to speaking and listening, suggest that teachers will have a confident understanding about the way language works. The National Curriculum requirement for knowledge about language in all the Programmes of Study (Department for Education (DfE) 1995a) made many teachers uneasy. The subsequent curriculum for ITT (DfEE 1998a) has a very clear focus on developing trainees' own knowledge about language and since 1998, the NLS has ensured that practising teachers have received detailed and updated guidelines and more practical classroom support for the development of initiatives, such as *Grammar for Writing* (NLS 2000b) and *Developing Early Writing* (NLS 2001).

It is now acknowledged that in the primary years children's knowledge about language use and structure should be developed more systematically (Bunting 2000: 19). In order to do this, teachers must also feel confident about the aspects of language that they will need to teach, understanding the structure of both spoken and written language and the way these relate to the teaching of reading, writing and speaking and listening. For many, this may mean revisiting knowledge which is almost certainly implicit or taken for granted and making it explicit; reassuring yourself that you know and can use appropriate terminology and understand how it relates to your teaching.

Making implicit knowledge (which all speakers of a language possess) explicit, is an important aspect of English work in speaking and listening in the later primary years:

> Opportunities for talking about and studying language need to be ensured. These can occur in the normal, everyday work of the classroom – we need to be alert to such opportunities and to exploit them. I call these incidental opportunities. But there is a need to provide also for more focused and sustained attention to language, to set up activities, projects, sessions, where language is the central purpose. Language must take its place as part of the content of the English curriculum beyond the confines of the literacy hour.
> (Bunting 2000: 20)

The requirements for courses in ITT (DfEE 1998a and revised version 2002) emphasise that trainees should feel confident enough about their own knowledge and understanding to ensure that pupils progress from, 'their implicit knowledge of how language works, to understanding it explicitly so they can evaluate how they and others write and speak' (DfEE 1998a: A.1.a.). As far as Speaking and Listening is concerned, you should be able to help pupils progress from an informal and personal use of language, the language of their home and everyday life, to being able to use more language in formal and impersonal ways, being able to adapt to the needs of different audiences and being in control of a variety of forms of language. These requirements reiterate and mirror the requirements for pupils' knowledge and understanding of language in the National Curriculum, but the emphasis is on teachers' knowledge and understanding of the nature of this progression and how it may best be achieved.

With reference to speaking and listening, DfEE (1998a: 3.A.i–iv) stressed that this progress depends on, the 'early and continuing experience' of:

i.   spoken language in a wide variety of contexts for different purposes
ii. language sounds, structures and patterns that come from extensive exposure to oral language, and the relationship between these and written texts
iii. hearing, discussing, retelling and inventing stories and recounting and describing events; and on their understanding of
iv. how spoken language is related to written language . . .

The key words here are 'experience' and 'understanding' and they underpin the more detailed knowledge that must be applied to the teaching of reading and writing. Pupils' experience of listening to spoken language is crucial when you are teaching phonic skills, for example, when you want the children to 'identify and blend phonemes into words' (DfEE 1998a: B.5.d.iii). Listening to and using spoken language are prerequisites for starting the process of learning to read by recognising individual words and moving through the process to understanding the meaning of whole texts. Listening to stories and non-fiction texts and playing with patterns in poetry provide the foundation for the more detailed teaching of reading. The ITT National Curriculum emphasises that reaching this goal depends on your pupils' earlier experience of a wide range of spoken language. But it is also dependent on your own understanding of the structure of written and spoken language.

Knowledge about language

The ITT National Curriculum stresses the need for planned activities 'which require pupils to be articulate, coherent and effective in Standard English' and wants you to ensure that your pupils can use a range of registers in different situations, listen attentively and participate effectively in discussion (DfEE 1998a: B.5.g.i–iii). As a class teacher you will provide a model for the spoken skills that you want the children to develop. Using your own oral skills as you talk to individual children, share with them in group and whole-class discussions, explore and extend ideas, you will demonstrate the kind of questions that you want them to be able to ask, the rules for turn-taking in group discussion and the importance of listening. As you read aloud from a variety of texts, you will demonstrate not only the use of standard English but the need for pace and intonation in order to convey subtleties of meaning. You will model the skills that they will need when they are working in small groups where you will require them to 'make critical and imaginative responses to aspects of literature and to evaluate the texts they read' (DfEE 1998a: B.5.vi.).

Speaking and Listening and the Literacy Hour

In the early stages of its implementation there was concern that the NLS framework was going to prove to be a straitjacket, that teacher talk, albeit pacy and interactive, in the form of question and answers, would limit children's responses. Corden wrote passionately of 'the shameful neglect of spoken language' (1999). Despite the claim that 'Literacy unites the important skills of reading and writing, it also involves speaking and listening which, although not separately identified in the framework, are an essential part of it' (DfEE1998b: 3), it was clear that the framework did not include Speaking and Listening in the planning of work for literacy. From the beginning the framework was to focus on the statutory requirements for Reading and Writing in the National Curriculum for English but it could be argued that it still contributed to the development of speaking and listening. Maureen Hughes (1999) challenged what she saw as the myth that the NLS emphasised reading and writing to the detriment of speaking and listening. She argued that because all reading and writing activities during the Literacy Hour would be built up in oral contexts this would provide opportunities for pupils to develop their language and cognitive skills through using a wide range of talk.

The ITT National Curriculum and the NLS framework are quite precise about the knowledge that you will need for the systematic teaching required in a dedicated Literacy Hour every day: an hour of direct instruction through 'well-paced, interactive oral work'. In the teaching of reading there is much emphasis on the systematic development of listening skills in the hour in order to identify and respond to sound patterns in language and develop phonemic awareness and phonic knowledge (DfEE/QCA 1999: En2 1a–e:18). Stories, rhymes, alliteration and word play help pupils to hear, identify, segment and blend phonemes in words. Listening skills have a crucial role in early reading. The teaching of writing also requires speaking and listening skills – indeed these underpin all successful writing.

Evidence from the evaluation of the early implementation of the NLS (OFSTED 1999) has shown that the teaching of reading was becoming more systematic and better structured and was leading to improved results in national tests, but that children were making slower progress in writing. As previously mentioned, the NLS has published two documents and sets of training materials to address this issue: *Grammar for Writing* (2000b) which connects sentence level objectives with teaching writing and deals with compositional skills and *Developing Early Writing* (2001) which focuses on the teaching of writing with young children. In both, the NLS emphasises the important links between talk, writing and pupils' cognitive development:

> The growth of competence in writing also contributes importantly to the broader development of children's thinking. The more context-free and explicit nature of writing helps children to become increasingly reflective about language. By structuring and restructuring ideas in writing, children extend their powers of imagination, learn to express increasingly complex, abstract and logical relationships, and develop the skills of reasoning and critical evaluation. This, in turn, feeds back into their powers of oral communication (NLS 2001:8)

Ways in which the features and nature of written text are affected by oral telling and retelling of stories are discussed in Chapter 3.

Talk for writing

Talk for writing is now seen as an important feature of the NLS, 'Writing should start from talking – discussion which helps to capture content and purpose. This needs to go well beyond simply providing stimulating ideas and should help children to capture the content, sequence and style of what they are about to write' (NLS 2001: 15). Teaching units stress the role of both oral language and reading in developing writing, 'much of what children need to learn about writing from story-structure to written language features and punctuation, can be gained from story-telling, shared reading, and the oral interaction stimulated by them' (NLS 2001: 25). Talk for writing is seen as a significant feature in all aspects of the Literacy Hour; in shared writing, independent writing and plenary sessions.

Provision for pupils who are not fluent in English

The National Curriculum has a valid concern that all children need to be able to use the English language for a variety of purposes if they are to have equal opportunity within our schools and society. However, for pupils who are acquiring English as an additional language (EAL) opportunities seem less than equal. The SCAA (1996a) document *Teaching English as an Additional Language: A Framework for Policy* addresses this issue, establishing a set of key principles. It makes clear the responsibilities that all teachers have for teaching English as well as subject content, 'the teaching of effective spoken and written English needs to be embedded in the teaching and learning of subject content' (SCAA 1996a: 7). It stresses that an aim in teaching EAL is to 'build on the knowledge of other languages and cultures' (SCAA 1996a: 2) and outlines the need to develop whole-school policies. The English Programmes of Study (DfEE/QCA1999: 49) allow specific attention to be given to the needs of EAL learners and provide opportunities for focused work on language. The NLS has provided specific training materials for class teachers for raising the attainment of minority ethnic pupils, *Supporting Pupils Learning English as an Additional Language* (NLS 2000a). The emphasis is on the importance of developing spoken English as a prerequisite for the development of all other skills.

A principle of the English Order is the requirement to interrelate work across Speaking and Listening, Reading and Writing, so that work in one area supports developments in another. For pupils learning EAL this principle is of vital importance. Reading and writing can enhance spoken English by providing visual models of the language, while the experience of hearing and participating in talk which is focused on texts helps familiarise pupils with the vocabulary and concepts they are likely to meet. Work that integrates the Programmes of Study assists pupils to make use of strengths in one area as a way into another (SCAA 1996a: 8).

The 1998 ITT National Curriculum addresses the requirement that trainees should be able to make 'effective provision for pupils who are not yet fluent in English' (DfEE 1998a: B.5.i.i–iv). It suggests that pupils should be given, 'ample opportunities to listen to well-spoken, Standard English and to engage in activities before being asked to make spoken or written responses'. This would seem to be a good rule of thumb for all children but particularly for those who are not fluent in English. By the end of their courses, newly qualified teachers should feel confident about the sort of activities that will extend pupils' spoken English and be aware of the need for careful planning that involves 'bilingual and other support staff and use of additional resources such as visual aids, talking books and dual language materials' (DfEE 1998a: B.5.i.iv).

Assessment and planning for Speaking and Listening

Circular 4/98 Annex A, Section B (DfEE 1998a) is concerned with the preparation of trainees for evaluation and assessment of their teaching and their pupils' learning in English. Their courses should ensure that trainees are confident about formative, diagnostic and summative methods of assessing progress. As far as speaking and listening is concerned, this will involve trainees in feeling confident about setting up assessment activities for listening to pupils talking and being able to make effective use of this assessment information in planning future lessons and sequences of lessons; recognising the standards of attainment in relation to the level descriptions for Key Stage 1 and Key Stage 2 in English and being able to judge levels of attainment. The assessment of Speaking and Listening is discussed in Chapter 6.

Teacher–pupil talk

The NOP not only increased our understanding of talk and learning as an interactive and collaborative activity, but also focused among others on issues of bilingualism, gender, teacher–pupil talk and the discourse of different subject disciplines. This takes us back to the snail transcript introduced at the beginning of this chapter that highlighted the need to monitor and listen to ourselves as speakers. There has been much discussion of the function of questioning in the classroom: we are all familiar with the kind of questions that require pupils to make inspired guesses about what the teacher has in mind, the questions that test whether they have been paying attention or remember information that they have already been taught. These are often single-answer questions of a closed kind that do not invite or require speculation but are necessary to establish a shared use of terminology or the specialist vocabulary required by a particular activity or subject. The teacher in the snail transcript illustrates this:

Teacher:	What is the snail doing with the bottom horns?
Susan:	He is feeling along the ground
Teacher:	He's feeling along, so what would you call the bottom horns, Jason?
Susan:	Arms? . . . No sort of . . .
Emma:	Legs?

Teacher: You think they're legs, you think they're arms. What do you think
            they are Jason, if he's feeling with them?

Jason: Feelers

This is a common strategy that is frequently used to establish the terminology that is being used in a particular curriculum area.

With the introduction of a ten-subject National Curriculum there has been a concern for more specialist teaching. The Speaking and Listening Orders specifically require that pupils should be able to use spoken language for a range of purposes: to tell stories, explore, develop and clarify, predict, discuss, describe, observe, explain and reason, ask and answer questions while working in groups of different sizes and presenting work to different audiences. Working in different contexts it is expected that they will become aware of the range of choices that they must make in different situations. Through speaking and listening activities they will begin to become aware of and use a range of different registers.

At Key Stage 2 there is more emphasis on making these choices explicit as pupils use grammatical structures and vocabulary that are specific to the genre or style used by different subjects. At this stage, they need to be taught more specifically how to organise what they want to say and to, 'use vocabulary and syntax that enables them to communicate more complex meanings' (DfEE/QCA 1999: 22).

Working in small groups has an important role to play in achieving this; through group discussion and interaction the range of purposes for pupils at Key Stage 2 should include, investigating, selecting, sorting; planning, predicting, exploring; explaining, reporting, evaluating (DfEE/QCA 1999: En1 10a–c: 22).

Teaching and learning: subject-specific language

The final section of the ITT National Curriculum deals with the specific knowledge and understanding of English that all practising teachers need, recognising that, the English qualifications held by trainees may not be sufficient to provide them with a systematic understanding of language and how it works, or to enable them to feel confident in those aspects of English which they have studied and which they are required to teach (DfEE 1998a: C).

It is particularly concerned that you should be able to use the correct language and terminology in your explanations to pupils and that this knowledge should inform the way you analyse and describe pupils' developing confidence. The document specifies the knowledge and understanding of English that should underpin effective teaching. To a greater or lesser extent, all these will affect the way you approach the teaching of Speaking and Listening.

Research has also suggested that younger pupils have been restricted in their access to more specialist aspects of the curriculum by the tendency of teachers to rely on 'narrative' and 'recount' modes of writing in the early years (Wray and Lewis 1997). It has been argued that the assumption that young children are most comfortable with a chronological, story-based approach does them no service when they have to take on more abstract concepts and retrieve information from books that are written in unfamiliar styles. Non-fiction texts are characteristically non-chronological and use grammatically different structures from those of narrative fiction. Stories tend to take place in the past tense and use active forms, 'Once upon a time' there 'were' three bears and they 'lived...'; non-fiction texts tend to use the continuous present tense and passive forms, bears 'are' four legged creatures. They 'are to be found in cold countries...' Familiarising pupils with these differences in the texts they are reading and writing will, it is suggested, help them to use a wider variety of texts (Barnes and Sheeran 1992; Wray and Lewis 1997). Hearing non-fiction texts read aloud and being encouraged to give oral presentations that require description and argument, for example, will help them to recognise that a range of different conventions and styles is required in writing.

The National Curriculum requires that from Key Stage 1 pupils should be introduced to a wide range of texts including print and information and communications technology (ICT) based information texts, reading for information in non-fiction and non-literary texts. They should also be encouraged to write appropriately for a range of different audiences and be able to organise and explain information.

The NLS recognises that moving from informal everyday language to being able to handle the discourse of the subject discipline does not happen spontaneously and the framework provides specific strategies that will enable pupils to cope with an increasingly wide range of non-fiction genre. In *Grammar for Writing* (NLS 2000b) there is a summary of the organisation and language features of non-fiction texts and units of work demonstrate how pupils may develop an increasingly sophisticated grasp of the grammatical structures required for non-fiction writing.

> Like the child's conversational learning of and through language in the pre-school years, learning in school can be seen quite largely as a continuing apprenticeship in discourse, as he or she participates in, and takes over, the different discourse genres – that is, ways of making meaning – that are encountered in various subjects of the curriculum.
>
> (Wells 1992: 291)

The children in the two transcripts that you have looked at are in the early stages of this apprenticeship. The younger group talking about the snails have learned the basic rules of collaboration; listening and turn-taking, hypothesising and speculating but they are using mainly cumulative talk (see Chapter 5) and will need more help from the teacher to use more confident exploratory talk. The 11-year-olds discussing a poem have come a lot further; they are handling and sharing evidence. Both groups had learned how to do this through experiencing this kind of activity in a variety of ways in their classrooms; their teachers had laid the foundations for them to be able to engage in the discourse of the specialist subjects they are going to be required to use.

Looking at the teacher's role

In the 1995 National Curriculum the subject orders did not address issues of language learning in any detail. It was assumed that the English subject area would be responsible for a broad range of skills that would be transferred to other curriculum areas. However, concern about the difficulties that this presented led to the publication of *Use of Language: A Common Approach* (SCAA 1997c) which outlines the need for a shared understanding about the role of language across the curriculum. The theme of this document is the role of language in learning and the extent to which pupils need access to the specialist concepts, vocabulary and particular uses of spoken and written English.

> As pupils develop their subject knowledge and understanding, they need increasingly sophisticated and exact ways of saying what they mean. Through this they can express more subtle distinctions and more complex ideas. To do so they not only employ a more developed vocabulary, but also a range of grammatical constructions and ways of conveying shades of meaning or stages of argument.
>
> (SCAA 1997c: 6; NLS 2000b: 154–5)

This is learned in a variety of ways: through the texts related to specialist subjects, through the pupils' own writing related to the subject and, chiefly, through the talk which is involved in the teaching of different subjects. The core booklet is accompanied by a series of leaflets for each of the National Curriculum subjects which suggest appropriate teaching and learning strategies and provide guidance on planning with language development in mind. A research project in the School of Education at De Montfort University (Bedford), *Children Learning through Language*, analysed ways in which teachers at Key Stage 2 teach subject-specific language (Sampson *et al.* 1998; Grugeon *et al.* 1998). The research found that younger children used everyday language and experience to explain phenomena that they do not understand; for example, a snail might be described as having a 'hat'. As they encounter more complex ideas they need to learn appropriate terminology. Teachers need to introduce the language that is particular to that subject. The research suggests that the learning of content in subject areas is a continuum that starts with pupils as apprentice members of a discipline. They have a tentative grasp of a subject which teachers will help to develop into confident, independent understanding. An initial analysis of the evidence that is being collected has begun to suggest ways in which teachers teach the language of a particular discipline and encourage the children to use it themselves.

An example of this happening can be seen in the recording of a Key Stage 2 history lesson where a Year 5 class are learning about the Ancient Egyptians. The teacher is introducing the class to the particular language and ways of thinking that they will need to adopt in order to understand and write about the topic. His concerns appear to be twofold:

1. to encourage the children's precise and accurate use of language: *What is it called when you ask for something?*

2. to introduce subject specific terminology: *Has anyone come across the word for making a mummy?*

At the same time, he is also encouraging them to use linguistic structures that are typical of the non-fiction texts they will use in their reading and writing of history texts. The teacher asks, 'Can somebody tell me something about the gods?' This invites them to generalise and respond in an objective way, rehearsing the kind of structures that they will need to use when they write what they have been learning about Ancient Egyptian civilisation. Their answers to this question show that they are beginning to use appropriate structures:

- Most of the gods had something they were leader of . . .
- To kill a cat in Egypt meant certain death . . .
- The gods were like a family . . .

In another lesson on the Aztecs the teacher introduces an important historical concept:

Teacher: OK. One of the skills you need in history is to use your eyes when you're looking at evidence. Now, can anyone remember what a primary source is?

Unless children understand the nature of historical sources, they will be unable to engage in the process of thinking like a historian; the teacher encourages them to ask questions and share ways of expressing a definition. Once they have collaborated to reach a satisfactory or specific definition, he is able to confirm their suggestion and develop it further:

Teacher: Absolutely right, it is something that dates from the time that you are actually studying – so if you're studying Aztec civilisation 700 years ago and you've got a statue that's about 700 years old, made by the Aztecs, that is a primary source, it's an important piece of evidence that you can look at very closely and perhaps draw some conclusions about.

He goes on to remind them about using evidence and how this leads to conclusions which are often hypothetical. By a process of questioning he encourages them to ask questions, make observations and hypothesise and consider the problems of the validity and reliability of their evidence:

Teacher: Supposing we found ten statues of Coatlicue in different parts of the Aztec empire and they all looked roughly alike, what would that prove?

Ben: It would prove that in every part of the empire, they're still praising the same god.

Teacher: Very good, it proved that they praised the same god . . .

Sophie: . . . and they thought that the gods looked exactly alike.

Teacher: Absolutely right, they all had the same idea of what the god looked like, so you knew that there were good communications throughout the empire...

Working with the whole class, the teacher uses questions to elicit and expand the children's knowledge and understanding of the process. He asks for clarification: *Can anyone add any detail to that? How do you know that?* He paraphrases and expands their ideas introducing new vocabulary:

Teacher: ...that they had human sacrifice, you mean? It shows something about their attitude to humans...

He introduces them to the possibility that a secondary source may have limitations: *Does this picture tell us how big the statue is? The book lets us down a bit there...*

Learning to use the discourse of a subject

It would seem that all subjects have their own ground rules or a specific discourse and that gaining access to these largely depends on the way that teachers organise activities for talk.

In the lessons we have recorded, we can see how the teacher models ways of behaving as an historian: he uses some specialist terminology: *source, evidence, problem, features, research, observation, detail, conclusions.* He uses the language of hypothesis and speculation: *supposing...who reckons it might be...? It's unlikely, but...I think it's probably...It looks as if it's meant to be...* He encourages the children to respond in the same thoughtful and tentative ways, *because it was quite important...It could be...I think it's quite big because I would have thought of the temples as being quite big...like, if you walk into a church...*

He engages the children in the process of dealing with historical evidence; encouraging them to observe closely, speculate and hypothesise about what they can see, to provide justification for their assertions and begin to use appropriate specialist terminology that is different from their everyday, informal language. They are doing this through what has come to be known as the 'joint construction' of knowledge:

An extremely important function of talk in the classroom is as a means for developing shared understanding. Through joint action and talk, participants in the process of teaching and learning build a body of common knowledge which provides a contextual basis for further educational activity. (Mercer, in Norman 1992: 217)

Valuing individuals

This chapter has suggested some of the issues that you will need to be aware of and think about as you plan schemes of work for Speaking and Listening. If you are going to help all children to participate equally in a curriculum that values oracy, there will be many more that you will need to take into account and often these relate specifically to individuals or groups in your classroom. For example, we need to be aware of and sensitive to gender differences in speaking and listening. By the time children come to school they have already learned how to speak in different ways according to their gender and their gendered identities (Swann 1992). You will need to take gender into consideration in your planning and assessment.

> By aiming to free children from the constraints of gender and taking positive steps to cater for the different needs of girls and boys as learners of English, teachers are helping to create opportunities for greater achievement across the curriculum for all pupils they teach.   (Browne 1996: 182)

There are also children who may seem to have a range of individual difficulties with oral language, those who are perceived to have 'poor language', those with hearing loss or speech disorders, for all of whom special strategies should be adopted. These issues will be discussed in later chapters as we look at strategies for teaching speaking and listening.

Conclusion

Over the last 30 years, what began as a specialist research topic on children's spoken language has broadened to an understanding of the interrelationship in learning and teaching, between speaking and listening, reading and writing. Oracy is now fully integrated as one of the three Programmes of Study for English in the National Curriculum. The pressure for change that led to this came from a curriculum project that was based in actual classroom practice where teachers were able to explore and reflect together. We hope that this book will encourage groups of teachers in training and in classrooms to continue to talk and reflect together about their experience and practice.

For the team writing this book, we have become more aware of the capacity of speaking and listening to be central to the objectives of a society that values life-long learning in a participative democracy. The process starts in the home with the development of the child's own language resources in social interaction with family and community, is promoted through constructive strategies at the start of formal learning (see Chapter 2), is recognised in diagnostic baseline assessment (see Chapter 6) and ultimately leads to the self-managing, independent, autonomous adult, confidently using language as a citizen.

Further reading

Bunting, R. (2000) *Teaching Language in the Primary Years*, 2nd edn. London: David Fulton Publishers.

Corden, R. (2000) *Literacy and Learning Through Talk. Strategies for the primary classroom.* Buckingham: Open University Press.

Goodwin, P. (ed.) (2001) *The Articulate Classroom. Talking and learning in the primary school*. London: David Fulton Publishers.

Mercer, N. (2000) *Words and Minds. How we use language to think together.* London: Routledge.

CHAPTER 2

Talk in the Early Years

Introduction: from home to school

I can remember when I first took a Reception class complaining to a colleague about the 'poor' language of the children in my class, 'Why, they can't even ask to go to the toilet properly', I grumbled. 'Well', Martin replied somewhat carefully, 'I don't know about you, but in our house we don't *ask* to go to the toilet, we just go.' Although my first reaction was to laugh, my inward reaction was one of mild indignation. My expectation, perfectly laudable, was that the child, after raising her hand should say 'Please Mrs Hubbard, may I go to the toilet?' As their teacher I was there to help the children, many from a deprived socio-economic background, to achieve and one of the best ways of doing this was to encourage them to speak 'properly' as soon as possible in order to reach the level of literacy that I wanted for them. On speaking to other Reception class teachers I found that their complaints echoed mine. We wanted the children to succeed academically and at the same time to speak clearly, succinctly and to the point, preferably in sentences, and with socially appropriate language. What we wanted was a culturally specific language reflecting our own backgrounds as teachers, and if the child did not match this then they and their parents were regarded as deficient in some way. Parents were censured in particular – after all where had the children been the last five years?

On reflection, I think that my colleague Martin's remark prompted me for the first time to consider the context of the shift from home to school for four- or five-year-olds and the language implications of this change of environment. In 1985 when I was teaching in Devon, I was keen to take part in a study of young children's talk at home and at school. As part of my preparation I read a book by Tizard and Hughes, *Young Children Learning* (1984), which turned out to be a critical event in my teaching career. I realised that my linguistic demands of the children were wholly inappropriate and that my knowledge of language development was quite inadequate. I began to realise that I knew very little about the home life of my children and that what knowledge I had was based on assumptions. It was only on visiting children at home and talking to their parents that I began to gain a more realistic picture of their language and the real language ability of the children in my class.

Aim of this chapter

This chapter aims to reassert the value and importance of talk, drawing on good practice by teachers working with young children in their classrooms. It is about speaking and listening being an essential part of the development of literacy. Teachers, particularly in the light of the Literacy Hour, do not necessarily have to change their activities radically in order to develop speaking and listening. What this chapter seeks to do is to help teachers revisit and reflect on the power of talk in day-to-day life in the early years classroom.

Talk in the early years

Any understanding of the way children and adults use language at home and at school must be grounded in the ways in which language itself develops and in the very nature of talk. You may find it useful to think of conversation and speaking and listening as analogous to a game of tennis. The talk itself is the tennis ball and the speaker and listener the two players. The server/speaker hits the talk to the receiver/listener who then becomes the hitter/speaker and hits the talk back to the server/receiver. This toing and froing continues until perhaps the ball falls short (a misunderstanding/unclear explanation), when one of the players has to reach out and retrieve it, before hitting the talk back into the play area/conversation and so the game continues. Talk between an adult and a young child is analogous to a game of ball with a toddler. The adult has to do most of the work running round and retrieving the ball (or talk) and practically throwing the ball (or talk) into the arms (or ears) of the less experienced player (or talker). I do not think it is claiming too much to assert that playing like this with a toddler is almost a natural reaction. It is Davies (Wilkinson *et al.* 1991: 111) who writes that 'speech is part of normal behaviour' yet this very ease and naturalness of use can lead us to underestimate its importance in language and learning. Talk is not like reading and writing, which are taught explicitly by teachers, having high status and being systematically recorded in the classroom. But we do not explicitly teach talk in the classroom and it is an arduous process to record and transcribe. It is perhaps the transitory nature of talk which makes it difficult to track, to assess and comment upon.

In the recent NLS publication *Developing Early Writing* (2001) one of the criteria for a successful writing classroom will include 'rich oral experience of telling, retelling and refining texts as a preparation for writing'. In a further section entitled 'From speaking to writing' the book then goes on to explain and demonstrate the differences between speaking and writing, briefly commenting on the interrelationship between speaking and writing and on the importance of talk in shared writing.

Talk precedes reading and writing and in order to understand the significance of this we need to go back to the very beginnings of speech itself. The use of unobtrusive microphones and recorders enabled researchers such as Newsom and Newsom (1975) and Shields (1978) to observe closely the interactions between mother and baby. Not only were their gestures and facial movements examined, but also the 'motherese' or baby-talk which adults often adopt when having 'conversations' with a baby.

Here is an exchange between a mother and her three-month-old baby. The scene is easy to imagine, as are the adult's gestures, facial expressions and tone of voice.

Ann:	(*smiles*)
Mum:	Oh what a nice little smile
	yes, isn't that nice?
	there
	there's a nice little smile
Ann:	(*burps*)
Mum:	what a nice little wind as well
	yes, that's better, isn't it?
	yes
	yes
Ann:	(*vocalises*)
Mum:	there's a nice noise
	(*Mother has been feeding Ann: she removes the bottle*)
Mum:	are you finished?
	yes? (*removing bottle*)
	well, was that nice?

(McTear 1987: 65)

In this transcript it is the mother's skill, her 'fine-tuning' (Bruner 1983: 39), which is making this interaction take on the appearance of a conversation. Such conversation-like interactions form the basis for talk. The actions and speech are not random but well synchronised and conform to social patterns such as questions and answers. In a review of theories of early language acquisition, Garton and Pratt (1989: 22) conclude that 'there is some propensity in the infant for language'. They lay particular emphasis on the adult being sensitive to the infant's gestures and early attempts at language. It is the adult tuning into the child's meaning intention who is developing the infant's talk; it is quite simply the adult assuming the infant is attempting to say something important.

Talk in the home

The richness of talk in the home has been well researched and documented, most notably by Brice-Heath (1983), Tizard and Hughes (1984), Wells (1987) and in the *Early Years Language Project* in Devon which started work in 1986. A typical transcript from this project reveals a four-year-old in conversation with his mother. The family lived in a dockland area of a major city and spoke in the local dialect. In this extract the mother is explaining to four-year-old Ross that he will be eating school dinners when he starts school shortly.

R: You do have to buy me a packed lunch box 'cos I go packed lunch.

M: Well you'll stay to dinners like Neil. (His brother)

R: That's school dinners.

M: That's school dinners like Neil, won't yer?

R: Yeah, an' you goin' 'ave to buy me a box.

M: Oh no, you won't need a packed lunch box if you staying school dinners 'cos they'll cook yer dinner in school an' give it to yer.

R: No they don't 'cos they 'aven't got a cooker.

M: They have.

R: You wouldn't know.

M: Yeah.

R: You gotta make it.

M: No, mummy don't make it, they make it in school an' then you sit down with all the other children an' eat yer dinner.

Later in the same conversation they are talking about Ross starting school:

M: Yeah, well, that's what you go to school for to learn how to write things down and how to read and how to spell, i'n'it?

R: You can't spell.

M: Can.

R: No you can't.

M: I can.

R: When you was four you couldn't spell.

M: No, that's why Mummy went to school, to learn, that's why you go to school, i'n'it?

R: To learn.

M: Mmm.

R: Did you go to school to learn?

M: Mmm.

R: You don't now do you?

M: No, don't go t'school now.

Ross and his mother are using the language of their speech community to further Ross's knowledge about school. It is an example of what Tizard and Hughes (1984) would call 'a passage of intellectual search', an example of speech they found to be all too rare in the nursery school. Ross, by making challenging statements, is trying to make sense of an important aspect of school life. His mother, in her explanations, is attempting to reassure him and clear up his misunderstandings about school dinners. Ross and his mother are communicating well and 'the basics' are there. What we need to remember is that home talk might well be different but it is not deficient. The Bullock Report, *A Language for Life* urged that 'No child should be expected to cast off the language and culture of the home, as she crosses the threshold nor to act as though school and home represent two totally separate and different cultures, which have to be kept firmly apart' (DES 1975: 286).

Discussion and comment 1

Is the language spoken in this extract different from what we would expect in school? In what ways? Perhaps you feel that there is a more even 'balance of power' between the two speakers. Because of the close relationship between mother and child there are more one-word answers and sometimes these are not conventional words, but ones they use when they are together. The child is exploring something that puzzles him. Would he be able to do this in a busy classroom?

Into school

Of course teachers cannot attempt to replicate the one-to-one conversation which happens in the home, yet if the 'basics' of communication are there, teachers are well able to build on these. The *Curriculum guidance for the foundation stage* (DfEE/QCA 2000) sets out its aims on language and communication in the Early Learning Goals and refers specifically to speaking and listening. By the end of Reception children should be able to:

- interact with others, negotiating plans and activities and taking turns in conversation
- sustain attentive listening, responding to what they have heard by relevant comments, questions or actions
- listen with enjoyment, and respond to stories, songs and other music, rhymes and poems and make up their own stories, songs, rhymes and poems
- extend their vocabulary, exploring the meanings and sound of new words
- speak clearly and audibly with confidence and control and show awareness of the listener, for example by their use of conventions such as greetings, 'please' and 'thank you'
- use language to imagine and recreate roles and experiences
- use talk to organise, sequence and clarify thinking, ideas, feelings and events
- retell narratives in the correct sequence, drawing on language patterns of stories.

Further guidance on how to achieve these aims is set out under the heading of what the practitioner needs to do.

Some of the key words from the communication, language and literacy section of the *Curriculum guidance for the foundation stage* (DfEE/QCA 2000) which we need to remember are 'develop', 'encourage' and 'explore' particularly when we try to address some of the issues which worry Reception teachers, such as the usages 'I bringed it' or 'I dided it'. This over-application of the past tense rule of adding '-ed' is a sign of a young child hypothesising and trying to fit the 'rules' to their own speech. And yet post-Reception there is a requirement in the National Curriculum (DfEE/QCA 1999) that 'pupils should be introduced to some of the main features of spoken standard English and be taught to use them'. We therefore need to consider how to address this.

There are various possible lines of approach. Listening to what the child says and then answering using the correct form is one way: 'I cutted my finger.' 'Oh dear, you cut your finger?' There is also direct correction, but this has little lasting effect and is extremely frustrating for the adult. A third and perhaps a more effective way would be to reflect on the varieties of talk in a lesson. A consideration of the different ways we speak in different situations could address the issue obliquely yet in a substantial way.

For example, a popular topic at Key Stage 1 is 'Ourselves'. A good starting point for this is for the teacher to bring in a photograph of herself as a baby and tell stories of her own family. The next step is for the children to bring into school photographs of themselves when they were babies and any toys, clothes or books that might still be in the family. Topics like this are rich in learning potential and often expand to include parents and other areas of the curriculum. Their great strength is that they build on the child's own background, knowledge and experience. It is important to focus on the spoken language and although a great deal of talk occurs naturally in an early years classroom, it is useful and fun to have specific lessons on talking about talk. You might ask the children to consider the kinds of language they used when they were very young.

- How did you ask for a drink when you were a baby?
- What did you use for 'thank you' and 'please'?
- What do you say now?
- How do you ask for a drink at school?
- How do you greet your friends/teacher/head teacher?
- Can we write it down? What do you notice?

It is important to write these down on a large sheet of paper in order to draw attention to the words or phrases. A simple table could be drawn up in order to discuss family words sometimes called 'idiolect' and their orthodox equivalents:

	1 year	5 years
mother	maaa	mum
father	daaa	dad

Such tables can be made more complex by the addition of more words and ages: they can be individual tables or a whole-class activity. The teacher with skill and sensitivity enables the children to reflect on their idiolect and perhaps on the wider issues of speaking and writing, for example, this is what we all *say*, but what would we *write*? Particular aspects that need to be addressed are adaptation to listeners and context and an introduction to some of the features that distinguish standard English from the patterns of speech practised so far by the child.

The issue here is that the children are talking about the language itself, they are learning about language through talking about language and acquiring a metalanguage. As teachers are surrounded by constant talk in a busy Reception class, it is easy to forget its importance; there's a danger of not giving talk its due attention. Speaking and listening are not incidental but require definite planning.

Discussion and comment 2

What would be our specific aims for speaking and listening in a topic on 'Ourselves'? You may have considered the following: reflection on our own talk, the differences between speaking and writing, the recognition of the differences in talk and what is appropriate at different times. Of course, any aims would also need to take into account the Programmes of Study.

News time

This is a classic activity in early years classrooms, with children gathered on the carpet in front of the teacher. It is used for an exchange of news, 'show and tell', story or the re-enforcement of a specific point the teacher wants to get across. Many teachers, believing it to be a time for children to express themselves orally, gave it considerable time. More recent research – the National Oracy Project (NOP) (1989–93), for example – suggests that news time in practice is often an opportunity for the teacher rather than the children to talk, and that its value for the development of children's talk can be limited. A variant of news time is sometimes called circle time which incorporates a more personal approach and encourages children to express their feelings on particular issues. Other observers (Housego and Burns 1994) question the appropriateness of this more personal form of interaction in the context of British cultural norms. And yet many are convinced of the value of gathering together on the carpet for the purpose of stimulating speaking and listening. Children are often bursting to relate a recent event or to show a new toy, and teachers need to give information while children need to listen. We should re-examine the usefulness of circle time and how it might be used more effectively:

- in pairs or groups, children can exchange news
- a 'jigsaw' (see Howe 1997: 20) in which children after hearing each other's news change groups and retell
- a feedback point, i.e. stopping the class in order to draw their attention to a specific item or to highlight similar events
- holding a much-loved toy while speaking.

None of these ideas is new but we need to evaluate what is perhaps a routine practice and try to discover the 'strange in the familiar'. In other words, we should re-examine the learning potential of news time and rediscover why the sharing of experience through talk is so valuable.

Discussion and comment 3

Can we think of other ways of using this time? What should the teacher's role be? Among your considerations think of the teacher as a facilitator, a listener and an observer. You might also want to question whether or not we are justified in asking children to express their feelings in public and what do we do if a child is reluctant to air their feelings?

Storytelling

My family recently had a 'gathering' of mums, dads, aunts, uncles, cousins, brothers and sisters. As with many other family get-togethers, there were the usual anecdotes: 'D'you remember when . . .'; 'When you were little . . .'; stories of wartime, holidays, weddings and births; the sentimental and the sad; stories of the family long ago – all slightly altered and embellished in the telling to make the anecdotes funnier, more memorable, to stake out a place in the family or perhaps to hold the floor until interrupted. Even as an active participant, I was struck by the recognition that we were all engaged in storytelling. These stories were not carefully structured, with a beginning, middle and end. They were all unpolished and repetitive; some were undoubtedly 'economical with the truth', while only a very few were delivered in complete sentences and in standard English. But what was happening here was the reliving of experiences, or what Andrew Wilkinson (1970) would call 'the experience of verbalisation and the verbalisation of experience'.

Through telling stories we were reliving our lives, trying to make sense out of experiences and to give a coherence to our lives – through talk. The centrality of 'storying' to our lives has been explored by Wells (1987), Chambers (1992) and Fox (1993), and is summed up in the conclusion to *The Meaning Makers* when the author writes, 'To try to make sense, to construct stories, and to share them with others in speech and in writing is an essential part of being human' (Wells 1987: 222). There will be further consideration of storytelling in Chapter 3.

In school children tell stories to each other, to their teacher, to the dinner ladies; stories of their birthdays, toys, baby sister or the tiny cut on their finger. These will be unpolished and unfinished, probably extremely short, but they are nevertheless the beginnings of storytelling. The teacher's role is to find and employ ways of widening the repertoire of the children to build up to more polished performances. We need to value their early attempts, create a literate environment in the classroom, tell and read them stories. Puppets can serve as a particularly useful prop in order to help along the telling of the story.

Puppets

The possibilities for talk, not just in the making of the puppets but in their presentation, are very wide ranging, and can help to widen the children's talk repertoire. Children for whom English is an additional language are able to use puppets as a vehicle for speaking in their first language as well as their second. A book is a useful starting point, preferably a well-known story so that the children can 'roam around the known', explore the story and make it their own (Clay 1979: 55). For example *Topiwalo* is a traditional Indian tale with a simple storyline. It tells of an old hatmaker who encounters a group of cheeky monkeys on his way to market to sell his hats. The monkeys steal the hats and the story goes on to relate how Topiwalo tricks the monkeys into giving them back. A dual language book can be useful in this context for highlighting similarities and differences between two languages. What we need to consider are the stages in such a topic, which might be:

- a reading of the story in English/community language
- looking at the differences in the writing of the two languages
- a retelling of the story in English/community language
- tape-recording the children telling stories in English/community language
- including a rhythmic or musical accompaniment, e.g. Indian drums
- telling related traditional stories
- making of simple puppets e.g. pea sticks and paper plates
- last, but not least, arranging a presentation to an audience.

The exploration of first language with bilingual children is important in order to give status and credibility to the first language and culture. This is important not only to the bilingual speakers but also the English monolingual children. The gains in confidence from any kind of presentation are crucial, but this might also be a presentation involving parents or classroom assistants. We know also from the work of David (1990) and Siraj-Blatchford (1994) that the encouragement of the child's first language has a direct bearing on the success with which they develop a second language. Furthermore, as the child grows in confidence in their second language, the balance between the two languages has the potential to provide further cognitive benefits (Mills and Mills 1993) and can lead to the development of interlanguage. This is a term used to refer to the child's own language system which develops through use and experimentation. This can also occur during the process of the movement back and forth between two or more languages which in its turn develops new knowledge and understandings. An issue for the monolingual English teacher is how to track and assess a child who is speaking in a language they do not understand. The use of other community language users such as teachers, nursery nurses, assistants and parents can be invaluable here. For example in the Topiwalo sessions the tape-recording in Panjabi was made initially for the deputy head – a Panjabi speaker – who at the time was off school because of illness and the purpose of the recording was to make him feel better!

Learning through talk may bring benefits in other areas of the curriculum. In the case quoted, the making of the puppets raised issues to do with art and technology. The range of talk involved in such a piece of work deserves analysing in the light of statutory requirements. Specific areas addressed include:

- telling stories
- participating in a performance, using appropriate language

- listening
- speaking clearly and with confidence
- a consideration of audience.

Making puppets also involves talk in relation to problem solving, including questioning, explaining, justifying, reasoning and hypothesising.

However, there are other aspects to traditional tales such as Topiwalo. Many of the traditional stories are highly moral and can be used as a resource to cover various aspects of the curriculum. Bearing in mind current OFSTED demands, we need to look at the wider aspects of such stories and how we can address important issues. The inspectors are required to report on the spiritual, moral, social and cultural development of pupils and how effectively the school teaches cultural diversity. These requirements are also echoed in the Early Learning Goals, particularly in the personal, social and emotional development and also in the National Curriculum. One way of addressing these demands is through story. A few examples of such stories which raise these issues are *The Six Blind Men and the Elephant* by Hester, *Fourteen Rats and a Ratcatcher* by Cole and Cressey, *Granpa* by John Burningham, *The Great Big Enormous Turnip* by A. Tolstoy (see Baumfield 1996).

Discussion and comment 4

How would a story address the spiritual, moral, social and cultural aspects of the curriculum? Can you identify the Speaking and Listening element? The list of books above takes into account issues such as a death in the family, working together to achieve a goal and listening to the opinions of others. For further work and ideas on story see *Start with a Story* (Sylvester 1991) and *Making Sense of a New World* (Gregory 1996).

Problem solving

'Investigations and problem-solving activities are efficient in helping pupils to apply and extend their learning in new contexts' (OFSTED 1995: 69). As teachers we are aware of this already but as it has been made explicit by OFSTED perhaps we need to consider how we can address it explicitly in the classroom. One way is through group collaborative talk (see Chapter 5). Collaborative talk in order to solve a science or technology problem is an example of children using talk in order to learn. Often in these contexts the nature of the talk is untidy, for example sentences will be unfinished, words repeated, and considerable interruptions will take place. Children need to be in groups for this kind of activity and it must be a task which requires them to talk to each other.

The classification game

- Give each group plenty of small pieces of paper and a topic each – animals, plants, food, TV programmes. Each group should not know the topic titles you have given to the other groups.
- Each group writes down examples of the category on the separate pieces of paper. For example, the animals group would write down the name of an animal on each piece of paper.
- The group sorts and then classifies the names. *You would need to ask the group why they have organised their examples in this way.*
- Exchange papers with another group. *Will this group classify differently? Can they guess the title I gave the other group?*

Discussion and comment 5

How would you bring this activity to a conclusion? You might find it useful to draw together the whole class in order to reflect on their decisions and relate the game to their current history or geography work.

The pin-eating animal game (See Figure 2.1)

This is a problem-solving activity devised by a BEd student at the University of Exeter, which again needs the children to work in groups.

- Give out the picture of the body of the pin-eating animal and the various feet, tails and heads to match.
- The children next have to decide which head, feet, tail are the most appropriate for the body of the pin-eating animal as he travels through the forest.

There is of course no right answer – which in itself is a learning experience – but the level of reasoning, justifying, speculating, hypothesising, specifying and persuading is considerable from this kind of task. However, this is an activity that is worth further exploration and analysis. Why would we do such a lesson in terms of the National Curriculum? The aim would be to widen the children's talk repertoire and improve their communication skills and an activity such as this would encourage the children to communicate effectively. They would need to choose their words in order to justify their standpoint and to learn the conventions of discussion, e.g. turn-taking. Through talk the children would develop their thinking and extend their ideas through discussion.

In 'Knowledge, Skills and Understanding' (DfEE/QCA1999) the headings of speaking, listening and group interaction would all be clearly addressed. The children would have to consider their audience, adapt their speech to the other members of the group and speak clearly. Issues of standard English and language variation might be brought up explicitly by the teacher. Under 'Breadth of Study' range is a key word and this activity would give the children the opportunity to talk for a range of purposes – for example, to explore, develop and clarify ideas, to predict and discuss possibilities.

We also need to consider other aspects which constitute good practice and which OFSTED would note, such as classroom organisation and management, differentiation, assessment, use of time and resources, and the expectations by the teacher of the children.

Best practice

This ensures that the teacher uses appropriate methods and organisation. In order to complete the activity and address the aims of the lesson children would work collaboratively in groups. Groups of no more than four would help to ensure all pupils are 'on task'. Setting a time limit is useful as it encourages the pace of the work. Resources are simple and require the minimum of preparation and explanation. Each group works without the teacher, leaving her to 'interact with pupils positively and economically' (OFSTED 1995: 70). At the end of the session the teacher will need to draw together the findings of each group via each group leader.

Differentiation and expectation

It would be the decision of the teacher as to whether or not to place the children in ability groups. Will the more developed child be challenged in a mixed or a similar grouping? Would the more timid child benefit from working with quieter children? Is there any way we could make the task easier or more difficult?

Assessment

One particular group or several children around the class might be targeted for assessment, or the teacher might be listening for evidence of a particular kind of talk in the class as a whole, e.g. hypothesising or standard English. How might this be recorded? Perhaps the teacher has a speaking and listening notebook or a rough notebook with a page for each child. If there is little evidence of the kind of talk the teacher wishes to target this will help to plan another activity which will address the teacher's aim. (See also Chapter 6.)

Discussion and comment 6

What would be the teacher's role in this activity? For example, as well as listening and observing, there would be times during the activity when you would need to intervene. The drawing together of the group discussions could provide a useful forum.

The Noisy Poems

This kind of activity can be done with a range of poems and is very useful, especially if the class has an assembly performance looming! While working with student teachers I have used poetry from the book *Noisy Poems* edited by Jill Bennett, which includes a wide range of noises from clanking trains and vociferous jazz bands to the softness of fish fins and the gentle sound of sampans in the water.

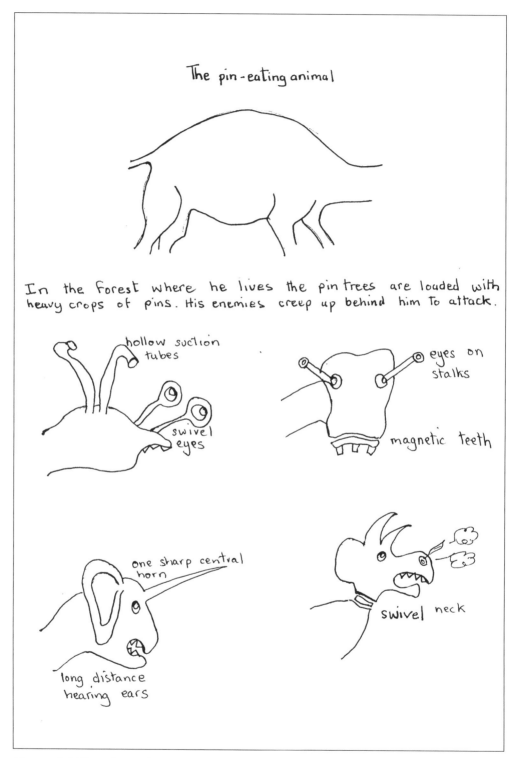

Figure 2.1 The pin-eating animal game

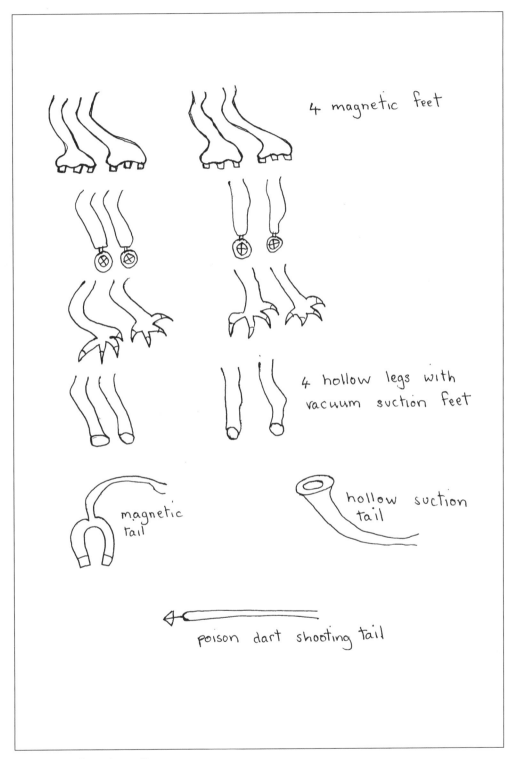

Figure 2.1 (continued)

- Give each group several copies of a poem, each group to have a different poem.
- Each group is to give a presentation of their particular poem. This will include actions and sound effects.
- Their first audience will naturally be each other, but if a performance standard is required then several rehearsals and refinements will be necessary.

This can be a noisy lesson! However, it is useful to reflect on the kinds of learning going on.

Discussion and comment 7

The head teacher is showing a parent governor around the school and the governor expresses surprise later at the amount of talk being allowed. How would you explain your lesson? You might for example refer to the National Curriculum and the aims of the lesson, but perhaps most importantly – invite the governor to the performance!

The child as a powerful thinker

A student teacher from De Montfort University, while working with Reception children on the story of Noah, asked one child where she thought Noah sailed to. The child with unanswerable logic replied, 'They sailed to Tesco, because they had no food.' Many a teacher has a fund of stories like this which are retold as amusing anecdotes and to illustrate a naive logic. This anecdote reminded me of the famous story of Laurie Lee who, on his first day at school was asked to sit and wait 'for the present', a story which illustrates how a child's misunderstandings can be funny, sad and perfectly logical at the same time. Yet this logic is also evidence of powerful and logical thinking at work in relation to the child's own cultural experience.

It was Vygotsky whose work taught us that the child has the capacity, with help, to develop ideas or concepts beyond their current level and that children are able to act and think with understanding of another point of view. *Children's Minds* (Donaldson 1978) was one of the books which first alerted us to the intellectual powers of the young child and was critical of the Piagetian view of the child as intellectually egocentric, a view which had a stronghold for many years over the minds of educators in early years classrooms. The work of Tizard and Hughes (1984) enlightened us further on the child as a powerful thinker; they describe children coming to terms with abstract ideas through talk. These powers need to be exercised and developed through talk in order for the child to gain control over their thinking and to make their thoughts explicit. The recent European Human Rights Act legislation of 2000 raised an awareness of children's rights and needs so that there are additional protocols currently underway which will amend the 1989 United Nations Convention for the Rights of the Child. Basically children have a fundamental right to be consulted on what is happening in their lives and in an article by Price (2001) attention is drawn to the work of Alison Clark and Peter Moss at the Thomas Coram Research Unit and Sterling Council Children's Service on consulting children on matters concerning their education. This will involve discussions with children on issues such as resources, their routines and activities. Obviously the young child does not possess the relevant experience and skills in order to make sophisticated decisions and long-lasting statements, but they can benefit by interacting with an adult.

Tina Bruce (1987) devotes a chapter of her book to 'The ability of the child to decentre'. Bruce explains that the child can empathise with others and is capable of understanding a point of view other than their own. Yet there are situations when the adult is needed in order to take the child further in their thinking: 'The role of the early childhood educator seems to be that of a bridge from embedded to disembedded tasks, from everyday meanings to situations beyond the immediate here and now' (Bruce 1987: 135). In other words the child is not intellectually incompetent but inexperienced. What the child needs is help to do things which they cannot do on their own.

Although children will display throughout the day evidence of their reasoning and understanding, it is also valuable to plan for specific activities for children to 'clarify their understanding and indicate thoughtfulness about the matter under discussion' (OFSTED 1995: 4). Specific activities might be:

1. Provocative statements displayed in a corner of the classroom can be used in order to encourage discussion, for example:
   - Children should wear their school uniform every day.
   - Children should only be allowed sweets at the weekend.
   - Children should go to school on a Saturday.

I have seen these titles put up in the writing corner in order to encourage argumentative writing after the discussion. Yet they can also stand alone as a talking activity.

2. Negotiating rules of behaviour in the classroom is a way in which many teachers encourage good behaviour. This negotiation through talk is meant to enforce good discipline in school through the children having some input themselves. Another aspect of this can be the children negotiating 'rules of talk' in the classroom (see Chapter 5). This is another useful way of talking about talk and of reinforcing positive and appropriate rules of conduct.
3. Stories can be a useful bridge. 'Well-chosen stories and sensitive discussion of incidents that arise in school or outside it may be also used to help children distinguish right from wrong behaviour' (OFSTED 1995: 84). Moral tales such as *Aesop's Fables* have long been used by teachers in order to instil good behaviour in their pupils, but we can and should broaden out these discussions to include moral issues of the day. There are a host of stories and books which can act as starting points or springboards for this kind of activity – furthermore, they can raise issues in an accessible way, often through humour.

Particular works and authors to note are:

- Anthony Browne, especially *Gorilla* which encourages children to 'read' the pictures.
- John Burningham's *Would You Rather?* encourages children to think and reach a decision.
- The poems of Charles Causley, such as *I Saw A Jolly Hunter* and *My Mother Saw a Dancing Bear*, raise issues such as hunting and cruelty to animals.
- Jan Ormerod's *Chicken Licken* is a delight, a picture book incorporating two stories.

Other authors/titles and topic areas

J. Baker	*Window.* Environmental issues
S. and J. Berenstein	*He Bear, She Bear.* Looking at gender roles
Anne Fine	*Bill's New Frock.* Gender roles
Michael Foreman	*Dinosaurs and all that Rubbish.* Environmental issues
Hoffman and Binch	*Amazing Grace.* Gender and race
Pat Hutchins	*Rosie's Walk.* Survival issues
Arnold Lobel	*Owl at Home.* A collection of apparently humorous stories which have deeper meaning. *The Frog and Toad Stories* which explore friendship
Jenny Wagner	*John Brown, Rose and the Midnight Cat.* Issues of jealousy

Questions

We need to be flexible to children's responses to a story yet, because of our awareness of the importance of talk, we also need to plan some of the questions we could ask. This planning would avoid the trap of asking questions such as, 'What colour is the cat?' or 'How many elephants can you see?' These questions have their place, but they are closed questions and unlikely to stimulate thinking.

Much of this chapter deals with how the teacher can help to develop the children's speaking and listening but, as described below, the teacher is not always as helpful as we might hope! When first exploring the possibilities of talk, I had to complete a task which involved me in tape-recording children and myself. I duly set up a series of short science experiments with two seven-year-old boys in the school's medical room, and left them alone with the tape recorder. What follows is a part of the conversation between Steven and Martin without the teacher present:

M: Water level is going up.
S: Yeah.
M: Going up all the time. (Reading) What happened to the level of water? Why has this happened?

S: I know, 'cos those are too heavy and . . .

M: . . . water and . . . marbles have taken up the room and the water goes higher

S: Yeah.

M: From the water level.

S: Yeah.

The teacher enters the room to check on Steven and Martin.

T: How d'you know that one goes in first?

S: Miss it's too big.

T: And that one's next . . . how d'you know?

S: Miss, I don't know.

T: You don't know?

S: No miss, I just . . .

(a lengthy silence follows)

T: OK. So what was he using then? He was using his fingers.

S: Yes miss.

T: And that's your sense of what? It's your sense of . . .

S: Humour.

T: Sense of humour? Well, could well be. It's your sense of touch, isn't it?

S: Yes.

My crass questioning here can partly be excused by my being a novice to speaking and listening as a vehicle for learning. On reflection I think I needed a few guidelines, such as opening questions of the type 'Can you tell me what you have been doing?' Then, of course, I should have been listening to the child. This might sound obvious to many, but during the course of a busy day in the classroom it is easy to forget, especially as talk is the easiest, most used and most accessible form of communication.

The help that teachers give to children in order for them to learn is often called scaffolding, a term coined by Bruner. But Eve Gregory (1996: 21) warns us that, as learning is different across cultures, so the scaffolding we provide should also take account of this difference. Cathy Nutbrown (1994: 75) in discussing the role of the teacher writes:

> Part of the responsibility of teachers and other educators is to ensure that children hear a wide range of talk and terminology and can therefore generate the words they need to be able to talk about their own findings and communicate their important and developing ideas through language.

Discussion and comment 8

Take some of the books from the list above and try to think of some questions you might ask your class. *Tell me*, by A. Chambers (1992) is a useful resource on which to base your questions and below are some suggestions adapted from his book:

- Could you present this book/activity to the class? How?
- What will you tell your friends about this book/activity?
- What kind of book/story did you think it was going to be?
- What is the most important thing about this story/activity?
- Would you like to read/do this again? If yes: would you read/do it differently?

Language play

Rhyme has long been regarded as a key tool in developing children's literacy, but the work of Bryant and Bradley (1985), and Goswami and Bryant (1990) have alerted us to the importance of rhyme in phonological awareness, that is the ability to reflect on sounds in words. What has developed from this work is the need to be explicit in drawing children's attention to rhyme, the sounds of words and their spelling.

Playing with the sounds of rhyme is the beginning of sound awareness in young children. My Reception class used to love *Mrs Wishy-Washy* from the Storychest Series and would often chant 'wishy-washy, ishy-oshy, pishy-poshy' or variations thereof. One of the joys of Michael Rosen's *We're Going on a Bear Hunt* is the 'splash! splosh!' and the 'swishy! swashy!' accompanied by appropriate actions. The poetry and playfulness of language, the 'savouring' (Beard 1995: 7) of the sounds of the words in the mouth is of principal importance in the early years. This leads on to the more sophisticated play on language encountered in Margaret Mahy's books. But do we make explicit the pleasure of the aunt's 'delicious rumblebumpkins' in *The Horrendous Hullabaloo* or the magical feel of 'the drift and the dream of it, the weave and the wave of it, the fume and foam of it' from *The Man Whose Mother was a Pirate?* The exotic names such as Novosti Krovsky in John Burningham's *Where's Julius?* or the seemingly nonsensical 'zoodle oop, little Zog' from Sarah Williams' *Good Zap, Little Grog* also provide a source of pleasure as well as the beginnings of sound awareness. But apart from an exaggerated reading or rereading of some of the passages, I would not attempt to explain away the enjoyment.

The rhythm and the repetition found in much early years poetry also helps along the sound. Early examples of this are the nursery rhymes children hear from a very early age. A later example might be Clive Sansom's *The Song of the Train*. It would be extremely difficult not to be carried away – linguistically speaking – by the 'clickitty clack, clickitty-clack, this is the way we begin the attack'.

Tongue-twisters are another form of language play and they can be exploited to draw attention to initial sounds. Children enjoy the alliteration and can invent them easily. Alphabet dictionaries on a variety of themes can be made with children, e.g. Alex adores apples, Balbir bakes biscuits, Colin cooks cakes, etc. Other early encounters with language play are the playground rhymes that have been collected in works such as Opie and Opie (1959).

The chanting in the playground of the somewhat aggressive:

I'm the king of the castle
Geroff! You dirty rascal!

to the rather more gentle

Oh, I'm a little Dutch girl a Dutch girl a Dutch girl
Oh, I'm a little Dutch girl from over the sea.

The appeal of the strong rhythm, the rhyme, the easy repetition and the downright subversiveness (see Grugeon 1988) of these playground chants might appear obvious, but these early experiences are valuable. They give children an introduction to aspects of literature and it is this combination of rhyme, repetition and rhythm that helps the sound of the language to become memorable and form a basis for literacy.

Other authors/titles

V. Aardema	*Bimwili and the Zimwi.*
Lynley Dodd	*Hairy Maclary from Donaldson's Dairy.*
Wanda Gag	*Millions of Cats.*
Gail E. Haley	*A Story, A Story.*
Dr Seuss	*Fox in Socks.*

Rhyme and rhythm

Working with rhyme is a long-established part of the experience of young children in the development of literacy. It is perhaps the particular work of Goswami and Bryant (1990) that has highlighted the importance of aspects of rhyme such as onset and rime. These are linguistic terms and are explained in Goswami (1994). Put simply, a syllable can be divided into two units: the onset and the rime. The onset in the syllable is the initial consonant(s). The rime is the vowel(s) and any following consonants in the syllable. The following table (adapted from James 1996) explains this further.

Word	Syllable	Onset	Rime
cat	cat	c	at
stream	stream	str	eam
midnight	mid	m	id
	night	n	ight

Before children begin school they have an awareness of rhyme that can be used as a resource in learning to read through work on onset and rime. A good beginning can be poetry, e.g. Chicken and chips (Anon) from *A Packet of Poems* (Oxford University Press 1982).

Chicken and chips,
Chicken and chips,
Everyone here likes chicken and chips.
We eat them all day
Never throw them away
We all like chicken and chips.

Read the children the whole poem asking them to join in and then invent other words to rhyme with chips. One class in a 4+ unit came up with *hips* and *chips* and *whips* and *chips* which were then inserted into the poem.

Teachers who have the confidence to rap can also reinforce the rhyme and the rhythm by rapping a story. *Rockpool Rap* (R. Hunt) from the Oxford Reading Tree Series is a good one to start with, although it does need practice! One adventurous student teacher, Karen, rapped *Noah Built an Ark One Day* by Colin and Jacqui Hawkins and went on to do a series of lessons based on the book. A more detailed account of this student's work with a Reception class follows.

A case study

1. The objectives for the sessions were to:
   - listen attentively to a story
   - demonstrate a recognition of the rhyming words
   - share an enthusiastic response to the text
   - interact with the text by active involvement
   - demonstrate an awareness of a grapheme/phoneme connection
   - show an awareness of how texts are constructed
   - have fun.
2. Karen chose the book *Noah Built an Ark One Day* because:
   - it is a simple repetitive story
   - it uses alliteration and rhyme
   - it follows a progressive sequence
   - the illustrations are layered and amusing and a good resource for questions
   - the story of Noah was familiar to the children.

The first session

Karen began by slowly tapping out a consistent beat and repeating 'it's raining' until the children became silent and listened. The development of routines, especially if rhyme and rhythm can be incorporated, is useful, not least for capturing the children's attention and this is an activity in which the children can join.

Next the book was 'read' as a rap, placing emphasis on the repetition and rhyme. Then the story was repeated, omitting the rhyming words. Quite spontaneously the children provided them. As the story was being read the children began to beat out the rhythm, but observed by the student were children who were 'out of sync' with the others in the class. A mental note was made of those children who required further rhythmic activities. One child read the story to the rest of the class who helped him to recall the rhymes in the story.

It is perhaps worthwhile to consider the assessment indicators of this first session. They were for the children to:

- sit quietly and listen attentively
- volunteer rhyming words
- demonstrate ability to beat out a rhythm
- recall a sequence of events.

In the evaluation Karen noted the four children who had been unable to 'hold' the rhythm. Otherwise this had been a highly successful session.

The second session

This happened in the afternoon when the younger children went home. The aim was for the children to internalise the story by sharing a response to the text, with the student building on the listening and participatory skills from Session 1. The story was 'read' again and the children were asked questions, such as:

- Why do you think Noah took the animals on his ark?
- What do you think the animals did all day aboard the ark?
- Tell me more about Noah.
- What do we know about doggy?

Drawings were made on sheets which had rhyming couplets from the story and children were encouraged to read these. It was while discussing the text again that ideas and concepts were drawn out of the text. Concepts were discussed such as kindness, rudeness, and cooperation: 'Noah was kind because he rescued the animals and the pig was rude for calling the hippo "fat".' The drawing task also allowed for the teacher to interact with individual children. Finally the book was looked at again in order to consider some of the conventions of print through questions such as 'Who is the author/illustrator?' 'Where do you begin to read a book?'

The third session

The aim of this session was to extend the young readers by active involvement with the text through performing the story of Noah. The children read their 'lines' from the sheets containing the rhyming couplets they had drawn on earlier, even 'rapping' their own lines. They swapped over sheets to play different roles and in some cases the children adopted different voices for different characters.

In conclusion

This was obviously a valuable learning experience for the student as well as for the children. Although Karen's work was part of an assignment on reading, speaking and listening played a key role in these sessions. As well as learning about rhyme and rhythm, performing, discussing issues, and learning the 'rules' of discussion, the children experienced the sheer pleasure and joy of playing with the language. The learning took place through talk which was a vehicle for learning about literacy, while the children were also learning about talk itself.

Other authors/titles

Alan Durant	*Mouse Party.*
Colin and Jacqui Hawkins	*Mr Bear's Aeroplane.*
Margaret Mahy	*When the King Rides By.*
Rosemary Wells	*Noisy Nora.*
Storychest Series	*Smarty Pants.*

Listening

Often in a busy classroom, what we mean by listening is children listening to our instructions and carrying them out promptly. Of course this kind of listening is significant, yet listening is also part of the interactive nature of talk. Activities to improve children's listening skills, sometimes produced to complement a reading scheme, might ask children to detect one sound from another. Their value needs to be considered carefully. Are they testing hearing or memory only? Listening corners are being developed now in classrooms to include a tape recorder and a selection of tapes of stories or songs for the children to listen to. The importance of these is that they encourage children to interact and are based on children using their imagination in listening. They also provide different models of listening which move beyond the purely instructional listening that can become the exclusive mode in the busy classroom. We need to put children in situations in which they are invited to listen and respond. Role play is one such situation.

Role play

This is a complex form of play and is sometimes referred to as 'fantasy play' or 'socio-dramatic play' in which children pretend to be Mummy, Little Red Riding Hood, or Doctor with the house or home corner being the usual context in which role play takes place.

Free play

Free-flow fantasy play, important as it is, does not necessarily engage the children with each other or lead to the development of language. Children are often left to play on their own and this is important. Often in their play they will be Mummy or Daddy yet they are not just imitating adults – they are, in these pretend situations, preparing for and rehearsing real life. The teacher will have set up the shop or cafe in the house with the help of the children, but the pretend game is theirs; they have ownership and the leeway to initiate a situation.

In one Reception class Abida, Razia and Joanne were playing in the house. They had taken saris from the dressing-up box and helped each other on with them before going into the kitchen part of the house. They discussed what they were going to cook, talking together in Panjabi, at the same time repeating what they were saying in English so that Joanne would understand what they were going to do. They proceeded to make chapatis using the actions of mixing and patting of the dough they had observed at home. They then pretended to fill a pan with water and, after putting it on the stove, they 'filled' the pan with what they decided was rice. During this activity they talked together about what they were doing, moving from Panjabi to English and back as they discussed with Joanne what they were doing.

This activity is an example of the way in which observing and noting children's free play can provide us with important information about the cognitive, linguistic and social skills which children are manifesting and developing in their play. The cooking represented for Abida and her friends an important link between the worlds of home and school, enabling the children to develop skills in school which they had practised and observed at home. This helps to give relevance to their learning in school. The children with English as an additional language, in moving from Panjabi to English and back for the sake of their English friend, were providing important evidence not only of their linguistic skills as bilingual learners, but also of their ability to use the appropriate language on the appropriate occasions. These children were certainly showing a knowledge of what language is about.

The important lesson here is: don't ignore play, observe it and look for opportunities to develop it and the talk arising from it. Children's play can convey information about their knowledge and understanding of the world around them. Yet we also need to ensure the children are engaged in contexts which require them to communicate and collaborate. Self-maintaining statements such as 'I'm going to be the baby now' do not constitute the interactive talk which is required in role taking. Adult intervention in play can provide an environment in which children have the opportunity to collaborate and interact with a more experienced language user. This can be achieved by observing the children's play and looking for opportunities to join them and develop what they are doing.

Adult intervention

We might next revisit the class shop and recall its value in imaginative play. The area has been turned over to a shop, with posters around proclaiming bargains or advertising the best brand to buy. Some of these have been begged from a local store, some have been made by the teacher and others by the children. The money is in a pretend cash till which is flanked by a table containing empty packets of food, plastic bottles, pots of creamy desserts, etc. One child is behind the table being the shopkeeper and another is arriving at the shop, carrier bag over one arm, while helping along her 'baby' with the other. This scene is a common one in many early years classrooms.

The children will have been playing in the class shop for several days. The teacher will want to extend the activity and relate their play to their real-life experience of shopping in order to give them the opportunity to find the words to give their experiences meaning. The teacher can provide a starting point for taking the talk further by asking the children about their real-life shopping. She might ask them what they are buying, where they are going, who they are going with, what they do when they return home. On the other hand, the teacher might want to intervene directly in their play and there are several ways in which she can do that:

- Will the adult enter the shop and ask for directions to the Post Office?
- Will she introduce a time limit to customers – this shop is closing in five minutes?
- Will she pose a problem – 'What can I have for tea tonight?' 'What can I make with what I have bought?'

The adult needs to think about how she can enrich and deepen the play, to engage the children in a variety of talk and yet not to take over the shop! This will require sensitivity and forethought in order to provide what Neelands (cited in Moyles 1994: 97) calls the 'subtle tongue' of the teacher. This last point is worth considering further. Do we have a *laissez-faire* approach in the classroom or a didactic one? I do not believe it is a case of either/or, for both of these methods have their value and teachers recognise this.

However, there is an additional approach to teaching and learning grounded in the teacher looking for, and taking advantage of, opportunities to intervene in the child's activities – not to instruct, but to collaborate with the child in order to facilitate their learning. In this way, the educator needs to be on hand in order to assist the child and help reinforce understanding. The teacher needs to recognise the 'teachable moment' in order to intervene (Woods and Jeffrey 1996). The difficulty, given the limited time for observation and listening teachers have at their disposal, is having the relevant information about what the child already knows and thereby engaging in a conversation that helps the child to develop their knowledge further. In order to provide opportunities for these kinds of conversations, finding ways of helping children to become more independent in their learning environment can enable the teacher to give more time to observing and listening and to recognise and take advantage of the 'teachable moment'. There is of course no one answer to this difficulty and every teacher has a different solution. One might usefully examine the classroom environment. Does it assist the child to become independent? Are teachers or their assistants too ready to jump in and do things for the child? For example, do the children know where all the equipment is or do they have to ask the teacher each time where to find a resource?

Discussion and comment 9

What other situations can you think of and what kinds of intervention can you plan? You could begin with the ongoing activities in many classrooms, such as sand and water play, block play or sharing a book.

Games

Simple games can be useful and fun, especially in an awkwardly short space of time, perhaps when waiting for the dinner ladies or a visitor to arrive. As teachers you will need to have a number of these games up your sleeves for such moments. Don't underestimate them – they are a useful part of the speaking and listening process.

Safari game
One child thinks of an animal and describes it feature by feature. You can vary the game and use a number of different subjects.

Who is in the bag?
Working with a partner, each pupil writes down a few names of famous people/characters on slips of paper. Fold papers and put them in a bag. Each person has one minute to draw names out of the bag and describe them to their partner. If the partner guesses correctly, try another until the minute is up.

Ring-a-ring-a-roses
Recite it first in a jolly voice and then in a scary whisper, with the movement to match.

Alphabet language
Using only the letters of the alphabet, tell someone off, soothe a crying infant, sell fruit on a street market or gossip to a friend.

Rounds
The second person begins when the first person has finished the first line and so on. Jelly on a plate, Boiled potato. (These can also be done to music.)

The parson's cat
The parson's cat is an angry cat, a beautiful cat. etc.

I went on my holidays
I went on my holidays and I took a . . .

Discussion and comment 10

What do we mean by listening? Why do we want children to listen to us and each other? Are there different kinds of listening?

You might be surprised at how much we require children to listen to our instructions! Think about a recent lesson – were the children listening to you and/or each other? Why were you listening?

Language diversity

Although this is a complex area for young children it is an aspect which we can begin to talk about in the early years. Raising awareness of the different ways the children talk is a starting point. Ask children:

- How do you greet your friends/head teacher?
- Do you speak differently to babies/grandparents?
- Do you have different words for going to bed/feeling tired?
- Do you have different words for kinds of food, e.g. sweets/lolly/toffees?

Reading stories and poems containing a variety of speech also helps to raise awareness of diversity, although some aspects of this last point perhaps need to be considered. Can or should we affect another dialect or accent? Teachers fortunate enough to have a varied language background can easily take on accents or a dialect from their own repertoire, for example, the Yorkshire tones of *Stanley Bagshaw* by Bob Wilson, but how desirable is it to adopt another accent when reading perhaps the Anansi stories?

Completing a language profile is a useful activity and promotes a great deal of talk about talk and the language we use. To begin with, it is worthwhile for the teacher to complete her own language history, using the following questions:

- Where were you born and how has that affected the way you speak?
- Have you moved and has that altered the way you speak?
- How has your education affected the way you speak?
- Does your accent reflect your social class?
- Do you vary your accent at all?
- Do you speak in a regional dialect, standard English, a patois, and do you vary your dialect according to the person you are talking to?
- Do you have another language that affects when and where you speak English?
- Does the way you speak reflect your age?
- Could you change the way you speak, and why?

These questions are taken from eastLINC materials (Smith *et al.* 1991).

An easy and enjoyable way to present your own language repertoire to children is to bring in a photograph of yourself as a child and tell them the story of your language.

Other authors/titles

John Agard	*I Din Do 'Nuttin'*. Poems.
John Agard and Grace Nichols	*No Hickory, No Dickory, No Dock.*
A. Ahlberg	*Burglar Bill.*
Tony Bradman	*Adventure on Skull Island.*
Dick King-Smith	*George Speaks.*
Kaye Umansky	*The Fwog Pwince.*

Conclusion

This chapter ends with the words of a four-year-old, Linda, who was part of my research. This transcript of a conversation with her mother as she is being put to bed shows Linda is able to use talk in a highly sophisticated way.

Linda:	I like you best.
Mother:	You like me best?
Linda:	Not when you shout at me.
Mother:	Not when I shouts at you? (*laughs*) You should be good shouldn't you? Eh? 'Cos if you was a good girl sometime I wouldn't have to shout at you would I?
Linda:	You don't like shouting?
Mother:	No, I don't like shouting at you and I don't like you being naughty.
Linda:	Don't you? Don't you think it's a shame when I cry?
Mother:	Do I think it's a shame when you cry? Sometimes.
Linda:	Sometimes you don't?
Mother:	Yes, sometimes I don't, 'cos sometimes you get sent to bed don't you?
Linda:	When I get sent to bed don't you care?
Mother:	Of course I care. Do you care?
Linda:	Care about you.
Mother:	You care about me?
Linda:	Every day.
Mother:	Every day?
Linda:	Even when I'm being naughty.

By their first day at school most children have learned how to talk and many of them, like Linda, in a very sophisticated way. That enormous development children have made in the first four or five years of their lives can now be given range, diversity and depth through systematic teaching in the early years classroom.

Further reading

Tassoni, P and Hucker, K (2000) 'Providing opportunities for Language and Literacy', in *Planning Play and the Early Years*. Oxford: Heinemann.

Whitehead, M. (1999) *Supporting Language and Literacy Development in the Early Years*. Buckingham: Open University Press.

CHAPTER 3

Developing Children's Oral Language through Storytelling

This chapter looks at narrative and storytelling as an aspect of speaking and listening that has particular significance in the primary school. The stories that children hear before they enter school have been shown to have a profound effect on their language and literacy development. Chapter 2 has illustrated and emphasised the importance of building on the language experience that children bring into school from their family and community and has suggested that much of this is in the form of stories that have been told and read to them. A study of stories told by pre-school children illustrates the power and importance of these resources: the 'narrative techniques that they have absorbed from their experiences of hearing written language' and the syntax that is necessary for complex thinking (Fox 1993: 116). The structures of the stories that they hear, and often retell, help them to anticipate the way stories work as they learn to read. Hearing stories read to them and sharing books with adults has been shown to be the best predictor of children's subsequent experience of learning to read (Wells 1987). However, we cannot assume that this experience is evenly distributed across the population; we cannot assume that all children will be able to transfer home learning to the school setting and be able to tell stories or cope with narrative structures easily and spontaneously. Research carried out over a year in a nursery classroom has shown the sensitive skill and understanding used by the teacher as she involved the class in narrative 'to such effect that by the summer months they are capable of sustained and coherent re-tellings of stories they have heard' (Dombey 1992: 2). In the process, Dombey describes how they learn a number of complex lessons about narrative which are relevant to their future as readers. We also need to be aware of the influence of children's out-of-school experiences: not only the stories that parents tell, but the games they play with their friends and the TV and video programmes that they watch, will affect their repertoire of spoken language and our expectations of their capabilities (Anderson and Hilton 1997). Drawing on and using these resources requires considerable skill and understanding.

Required to tell stories

Curriculum guidance for the foundation stage (DfEE/QCA 2000) **and** the *National Curriculum for English* (DfEE/QCA 1999) acknowledge the importance of recognising and building on pre-existing skills; the Speaking and Listening attainment target encourages the development of storytelling. The NLS framework for teaching (DfEE 1998c) reinforces this.

A major outcome of the NOP in 30 local education authorities (LEAs) from 1989 to 1993, was the emergence and documentation of storytelling as a significant factor in the development of oral language across the primary age range. The promotion of storytelling at this time has left a legacy of good practice (Howe and Johnson 1992; Grainger 1997; Grugeon and Gardner 2000) which has made a significant contribution to the English National Curriculum Orders. The first requirement at Key Stage 1 Speaking and Listening , 'Breadth of Study', is that the range of activities should include: 'telling stories, both real and imagined' (8a); 'Knowledge, Skills and Understanding', require pupils, to 'speak with clear diction and appropriate intonation; choose words with precision; organise what they say; focus on main points; include relevant detail and take into account the needs of their listeners' (DfEE/QCA 1999: 16). All these are skills which will be developed by oral storytelling and the NLS framework reinforces this. Text level work from Reception through to Year 6 includes oral storytelling: in Reception and Year 1 the emphasis is on developing understanding of story structure; stories may be re-enacted through role play and using puppets; oral retelling will develop understanding of sequence, character, dialogue and features of story language. In Year 2, role play and individual retelling will continue to develop this understanding which will become increasingly important to the development of pupils' written work. In *Developing Early Writing* (NLS 2001: 9) oral telling and retelling 'where they are helped to say it like the book' are seen as important ways in which children come to understand the features of written texts. In Year 3 an increasing familiarity with a range of traditional stories will allow more sophisticated discussion of typical story themes, characters and language and retelling will continue to make an important contribution to a more explicit understanding of narrative texts. By Year 5 'preparation for oral storytelling' sees this as a presentational skill in its own right (DfEE 1998c). This is also a skill that teachers need. The Literacy Hour requires teachers to model the skills they are teaching and to become confident storytellers themselves. This chapter tells how teachers developed this competence working alongside their pupils.

Reflecting on storytelling in school

We will look at the way a group of teachers in training came to recognise the different resources that children already had, and how they responded to them and developed them. These accounts reflect their own, as well as the children's, growing understanding of ways in which narrative may help children to make sense of a wide range of experiences while providing evidence of their developing competence in speaking and listening. In the edited transcript below, two trainee teachers talk about their experience of sharing stories with the children in their Reception and Year 1/2 classes.

Jan: . . . they were receptive to storytelling at any time of the day . . .

Val: We'd find that they were always willing to come and listen to a story and it was our main form of communication . . . if you brought them onto the carpet, telling a story, you were as one, sharing excitement, thrills, sadness, happiness, many emotions.

Jan: Yes, and many of the stories would spark them off and they would leap up wanting to tell you a story, something similar that had happened at home . . . 'Oh that's what happened to me', would come the cry and they would leap up one after another, trying desperately to tell you their own stories, which was a very exciting experience.

Val: And they found leads in our stories and went off and did other very creative things, they wanted to illustrate the stories . . .

Jan: I told the treacle one, about the monkey . . .

Val: Who gets, 'only trouble'?

Jan: I told that and many other African stories and the children would look at the words – *How the Lion Roars* described the sound the lion made – and the children were looking at whether the words described the meaning, they looked at the language . . .

Val: I was a bit worried about the monkey story, thinking my children were a bit young for it. I was concerned they wouldn't understand the African words but the children really enjoyed it and understood every word of it, though they did ask a lot of clarifying questions such as 'Why did he choose a prickly tree?' They asked a lot of questions to put it straight in their minds, but they enjoyed it.

Jan: But did you find they were able to retell the story straight away or the major incidents? I mean, there were children in my class who were able to tell back the story throughout the day. They were telling children in the class . . .

Val: Ah, that was something else, the storytelling corner I set up, I had two tape recorders, one with blank tapes and one with tapes to be listened to. This corner was used every minute of the day . . . the children were so prolific with their stories.

Discussion

As you read this extract from a much longer discussion:

- What did you think the students were discovering about storytelling in an early years classroom?

- What do we learn about their strategies as teachers?
- What contribution might these storytelling activities make to the children's literacy development?

Comment

The students were evidently surprised by the powerful effect of story on these young children; they discovered that storytelling was

- a means of communication and control;
- a means of sharing experience;
- a stimulus for other activities;
- a stimulus for looking closely at language;
- a means of developing expertise as tellers and retellers;
- a means for questioning and discussing issues.

At the same time they were extending their own repertoire as tellers, trying out a range of stories and providing resources for the children to listen and tell for themselves.

We can see how they are beginning to identify the different resources that children already have and consider how they can respond to them.

Becoming storytellers: a case study

The case studies we are going to look at are taken from written assignments by student teachers. They were required to prepare stories to tell during a four-week school experience and to use this experience to write an assignment. As they account for the strategies that they used they are also developing and making explicit the theoretical knowledge and understanding that will underpin their language and literacy teaching in future. The five students were all specialising in English on a Primary BEd degree. Their written assignment asked them to account for and analyse the outcomes of the storytelling that they had undertaken. They were not only expected to become storytellers themselves, to introduce and develop this skill with the children they were teaching, but they were also to develop a theory that would support a critical analysis of the work they had been doing. They had spent some time discussing and practising appropriate stories before they went into school but they all felt nervous about the prospect of oral storytelling. They all recorded their initial misgivings about storytelling. One student wrote, 'My initial response was one of horror and panic. I had never told a story to children before'; another described how, 'When story time arrived I remember feeling quite anxious, mainly because what I was about to do was quite new to me'. But their accounts show their developing awareness of the oral resources that both they and children brought to school.

One of the problems they all faced was the lack of models to follow. The status of storytelling in some schools was fairly low and few of them had experienced examples of teachers telling stories to any but the youngest children. It was not uncommon for students to report, 'Many of the teachers I had worked with did not even read stories'. Negotiating for time to do justice to work they had prepared was often problematic, 'It was difficult to make oral storytelling an important part of the curriculum because my teacher believed the proper time for stories was the last session in the afternoon which lasted for ten minutes'. You may find that this continues to be a problem; National Curriculum requirements have brought about tighter timetabling of the primary school day. This makes it harder to introduce approaches like storytelling if they are not part of the overall plan for a particular class. Some of you may have encountered professional storytellers in school or had the opportunity to attend local events which included storytelling. However, despite support from the National Curriculum for the inclusion of storytelling and encouragement to develop children's awareness of narrative techniques at Key Stages 1 and 2, it still tends to be a rare activity, especially with older children. Storytelling at Key Stage 2 is no less important than at an earlier stage, yet may be less in evidence. A professional storyteller, involved in research into the oral narratives of teenagers, described the scepticism that he encounters among teachers about the existence of a significant narrative tradition belonging to older children and the value of storytelling for older children. His experience of working with adolescents to compile an archive of, 'riddles, ghost stories, family lore, contemporary legends, local legends, creation myths, jocular tales, superstitions and personal experience stories', seems to contradict this (Wilson 1994: 3). Since it is unlikely that the examples that he is collecting appear suddenly when children transfer to secondary school, it is possible that there is a developing narrative tradition unnoticed in the playground throughout the primary school years. However, there was evidence of an embryonic narrative tradition in early years classrooms in the examples that the students recorded and wrote about.

Developing confidence as storytellers

Students found that it was easier to introduce storytelling in early years classes where there has long been a tradition of oral storytelling with young children (Colwell 1991). However, they were soon to discover that telling rather than reading is a particular skill and that once the printed word is abandoned the text becomes negotiable with the audience. As one student discovered:

> My first attempt at storytelling was *The Three Little Pigs*, because I know the story so well. As soon as I said, 'the wolf ate up the first little pig', the children were visibly upset, so I said, 'but he didn't, he went to the house of the second little pig'.

Moreover, the choice of story itself may have to be negotiated. Another student completed her carefully prepared version of *Little Dog Turpie* only to find that the class wanted to tell her about a local event that she was unaware of, 'Five days previously the chimney of the power station a few miles away had been blown up, the largest explosion in England for 20 years'. Most of the children had seen this event and the student gave up *Little Dog Turpie* for their dramatic demolition stories.

Once students had got over their initial nervousness about telling a story they were able to reflect on their delivery and the children's response. One wrote,

> Two differences which are immediately noticeable are the freeing of hands and eye contact . . . Freedom from the book facilitates increased eye contact enabling the teller and listeners alike to share the experience more directly. This close contact with the listeners enables the storyteller to gauge their reaction to the story more accurately, to pick out children who seem worried about the story and those that are not giving it their full attention. Freedom from the text allows the storyteller to deviate when needed to give a fuller explanation when something seems puzzling . . . Best of all, oral storytelling allows the teller and the listeners to create the story afresh each time (Wendy).

Preparing to tell a story

Students reflected on the need for preparation, 'The most important criterion for choosing a story is, do you enjoy the story yourself, as to prepare the story for telling you will have to become saturated in it'. One chose to start with a story she had known since she was a child.

> Nervously, but well practised, I set out on my adventure as a storyteller. To my surprise, I thoroughly enjoyed my first experience. Amazed at the deep, attentive silence which reigned over this very boisterous class as I told the story, I felt that the experience had really captivated them. Using my whole body in its telling, my hands, face even my eyes could express the story. Without a book, I felt that I was able to use my voice more expressively, concentrating on each word. As I told the story I realised that its shape was the most important aspect to remember. The details were unique to that particular telling and would change each time I told the story. I was pleased when even the most inhibited children began to join in the repetition, the children had become totally absorbed in the words of the story and so had I. We really enjoyed the experience, a fact that I had observed with delight as I watched the expression on their faces (Sue).

Before they went into school, the students had an experience of being in the audience themselves. A local teacher, who was a professional storyteller, came into one of their sessions to introduce them to Anansi the trickster spider (Hayley 1972) from the Caribbean. She talked about the importance of telling traditional tales and building up a personal repertoire of tales from different cultures. As well as making them aware of the potential for using props, magnetic and felt boards, puppets and artefacts relating to the story, she had reminded them how such stories can be a way of exploring real-life dilemmas; how they can 'transcend and unite cultures by depicting universal morals and truths' (Gregory 1996: 116).

The students had also joined a group of children at a dramatic telling of *The Hairy Toe* (Summerfield 1970) by one of the university's drama lecturers. Both sessions had helped to prepare them for their own storytelling; as one wrote, the first session had made them aware of the importance of, 'having at one's fingertips a range of folk tales from many cultures to use in today's multi-ethnic classrooms in order to broaden everyone's horizons'. The second session had provoked thoughts about the way a potentially frightening story might be handled, or mediated, by the teller. One of the students described how she felt that this had happened,

> firstly, the way the story was told, the 'virtual' nature of the language and the voice, committed the children's minds and senses and secondly, the emotion of fear was kept at bay by inviting them to become involved as participants and partners in the telling (Jane).

In this way, she had felt that 'the teller hands over some power and responsibility for the telling and this reduces the emotional fear'; the teller had maintained the listeners' involvement but defused the fear. She felt that, 'we do not generally fear that which we have power to control', and when she told the story of *The Hairy Toe* herself, she had hoped to further defuse any potential fear by getting children to model, paint and draw the creature the hairy toe had belonged to. In reflecting on the children's response to this story, she wondered about the effect of such a 'powerful genre' and suggested that these stories were using what Bruner has called, the 'language of consciousness' (Bruner 1986) and felt that this 'could have profound implications for the way in which children use language to express their view of the world'. She speculated that, 'as Carol Fox suggests, "whatever lies at the heart of storytelling lies at the heart of language itself"' (Fox 1988: 55).

Telling and retelling: the children take over

Becoming storytellers themselves was only the first stage of the process. The next stage was to enable the children to tell stories and for the students to analyse these stories. All were surprised by the quality of the stories told by children. Sue recalled that, 'It was the most unlikely people who displayed the most unsuspected linguistic resources and strategies'. A quiet boy who 'would often just nod in response to the register and never participated in class discussion' one day whispered to her that he had a story to tell and began, 'once upon a time in a country not far from Milton Keynes lived a little kitten called Tootsy', revealing a hitherto hidden ability to organise language and tell an elaborate story.

Sue taped the stories told by her class of 28 five- and six-year-olds. She had begun by telling short anecdotes about her pets, hoping that the children would respond with similar stories from their experience. She had expected simple stories but was surprised by the complexity of the narratives that they embarked on. Listening to the recordings that she had made, she was able to trace complex threads linking stories and observe how children seemed to be grappling with issues that bothered them. She comments on two stories told by Kerry:

Kerry: There was a dog and its name was Punk and it went outside and kept on barking, and it was one of them big ones.

Susanna: Dalmatian.

Kerry: Dalmatian, and it . . .

Susanna: Spotty dog?

Kerry: No, one of them ones with black and gingery colour.

Student: An Alsatian?

Kerry: Yeah, and it keeped on barking at everybody. All the little children keeped on getting scared 'cause it was that big. He had to go home and he got smacked and if he went near the food he will have no dinner for a hundred years . . . I can't think . . . or go to the vets and get killed.

Student: Oh gosh!

Sue commented, 'My final reaction shows that I was not expecting Kerry to end her story in this way. It was obviously, however, her way of coming to terms with what was uppermost in her mind. Her story had been a safe way of allowing her views to emerge. I saw Kerry still trying to resolve the obvious conflict in her mind when a week later she told me the following story about an incredibly 'good dog':

Kerry: A little dog what was good, and it was nice and kind and it was trained good and it gived people their food and it got the letters and it stayed on its own and it keeped on cleaning up everywhere and it was a nice dog and they said 'we're going out for a walk with you' and they took it for a walk and there was a big puddle – about that big . . .

Susanna: And it jumped into it . . .

Kerry: No, and then it . . . and it didn't get muddy and there was a big puddle with mud in it and it went round it again. Then they went round that puddle again and then round the big puddle and then they got home again and then it treaded in the puddle 'cause it didn't see and then it went upstairs 'cause it had . . .

Susanna: Have a bath . . .

Kerry: No, it had the mummy's slippers and then it took them off and then it went in the bath and then he cleaned the bath out.

Reflecting on these two versions, Sue felt that Kerry was trying to sort out a dilemma about good and bad behaviour, about crime and punishment. She felt that the stories were helping Kerry to develop her own views of the world and that, 'as Betty Rosen says, the story allows her views to "emerge safely"'. Moreover, it emerges with the help of her audience, Susanna, who is evidently listening intently, anticipating and predicting outcomes.

The importance of an audience, the social nature of storytelling, was remarked on by several of the students. Sue noted that in her class,

> the general standard of storytelling was constantly improving. Many of the children were incorporating facial expressions, speech and voice intonation into their developing stories. I was aware that this was actually being acknowledged by the children themselves. Many showing delight at listening to those they enjoyed and listening patiently and respectfully to those they did not.

Vicky tells a similar story of the children's growing confidence: 'the children I asked to tell stories were five- to seven-year-olds and had never been asked to tell stories before. In spite of this, they were not reticent but rather impatient for their turn to come'. Listening to her recordings, Vicky felt that, 'different types of story demanded different types of telling'. Two boys sharing a recollection of their trip to America, 'required an almost conversational dialogue in which one made a statement and asked for the other's affirmation of the detail'. Another pair of boys had told a fast-moving adventure story:

> The content of the story was fast moving in itself but the boys' voices became very animated as their enthusiasm and personal involvement increased. In places of highest excitement they alternated between teller and listener extremely quickly and with great skill. Their concentration on the story was so powerful that they were both totally caught up in the adventure.

In contrast, two girls in Vicky's class were, 'much more sedate in their pace', as they shared the retelling of *Little Red Riding Hood*, 'their close attention to detail slowed down the tempo as they strove to find the correct sequence of events and even dialogue', but at the same time they, 'used their voices to great effect, paying attention to intonation and the rhythm of the words'. Vicky was surprised to discover such awareness and confident use of different storytelling techniques in these young children. Another child had created her own style for a retelling of *The Three Little Pigs*. She did not attempt to produce a correct version but adapted the story in her own way. Vicky describes how:

> The brightness of her voice and enthusiasm for the story drew me and the entire class into a world of straw houses and puffing wolves.
> 'Can I have some of your sticks?'
> 'You can have as much as you like.'
> So he took 'em all.
> And when the class laughed at this point, she repeated the phrase in subsequent episodes, reacting to her audience as an experienced storyteller would. This was all the more remarkable since she was considered a less able child.

Indeed, some children seemed to have an amazing command of technique. Jane writes about a seven-year-old:

> His tale was fascinating, the story of a little boy who finds himself, having gone through a small door in a cave, entering a quite different world on the other side, a world of monsters. It was apparent that he was using visual clues to help provide details; for example, 'there was a monster school with monster chairs' (looking at the chairs) 'and monster music' (looking at the music stands). It was equally apparent that he was transforming what he actually saw into some kind of visual imagery, and that he could transmit such images to his audience. An interesting aspect of Toby's story was the monster teacher who spoke monster speak and whom the little boy could not understand. I asked whether the boy ever managed to understand, to which Toby replied 'No, never'. I was left to wonder whether there was an implicit message in this story. Bruner (1986: 64) says that 'the young child seems not only to negotiate sense in his exchanges with others but to carry the problems raised by such ambiguities back into the privacy of his own monologues'. Toby's command of devices to convey meanings and atmosphere and his grasp of the conventions of story grammar were impressive for a child of seven years. Perhaps the most linguistically mature aspect was the ending – 'It had all been a dream'.

Jane came closest, perhaps, to finding evidence of the existence of folk narrative of the kind identified by David Wilson in older children, when an eight-year-old girl in her class told a powerful ghost story. She was already a polished storyteller,

> using techniques of pause, different voices, varying dynamic and intonation, to create the type of breathless tension that holds a listener's attention. It was as though she was actually listening to someone else doing the telling, listening with an inner ear that directly informs the brain.

She told Jane that her aunt had told her the story and indeed, came to lunch at weekends and regularly told stories. When Jane asked how she remembered them she said, 'I read them out of my head'.

Intertextuality

All the students had found evidence in the children's stories of their dependence on stories that they had heard and read before. They were discovering that 'any story presupposes the existence of other stories...for both reader and listener threads of connection exist, threads of many different kinds' (Rosen 1984: 33). Most of the stories recorded bore out Carol Fox's finding in her own study that, 'The model for the children's stories was very obviously literary' (Fox 1993: 97). Kerry's stories drew on two stories that Sue had told the class. The monster story that Jane refers to has many intertextual references. Many of the children chose to retell familiar fairy tales. Wendy recorded a story told by a four-year-old as he was drawing a picture:

John: Now the elephant is on the ground.
          Now he's changed to green
          And when he was on the ground he changed to green.
          When the chameleon is on the floor it changed to green
          When it's on the floor this chameleon
          When when the elephant is on the floor
          it changes.
          Mrs Smith, when the elephant is on the floor it changes green like a
          chameleon.
Donna: No, it doesn't!
John: It does 'cos it's a magic elephant.
          There is the chimney and the smoke is coming out
          And it's nearly going to fall on the elephant,
          A changing elephant and when it's on the floor it
          changes yellow.
Donna: Oh!
John: I don't know what this is going to change into...

While this monologue might not seem to be a story, John seems to be developing a narrative structure. Wendy who knew where it was coming from, felt that it was most certainly a story: 'John has created an elaborate story around the previous week's tale of *The Mixed Up Chameleon* (Carle 1988), the drama of the chimneys and this week's folk tale of *The Elephant and the Rabbit* about an elephant who changes his appearance.' In combining real and fantasy events, Wendy felt that he had begun to create a 'possible world' into which Donna was beginning to be drawn.

Children learning to tell stories

Peter Hollindale (1997: 70) reasserts what has become a generally held belief when he claims that

> we construct our selfhood through memory; that we depend for our identity on our sense of personal continuity in time, and that we express this to ourselves by storying our lives ... we need stories as we need food, and we need stories most of all in childhood as we need food then, in order to grow.

However, such an assertion naturalises narrative and storytelling, and can lead to a belief that there is little for teachers to do other than provide the appropriate stimulus and context, and the children will tell stories confidently drawing on some pre-existing resource. As it was, this group of students found that they needed to work very hard with children who did not find telling stories easy. Jane reflected on children in her class who had needed help and drew on her reading of Jerome Bruner and Gordon Wells to help explain why this might be the case:

I noticed that he managed the opening and the beginning of the sequence very well but he became confused about how to describe his actual holiday experiences. In fact, this is no easy task since the capacity to construct stories from experience requires, a 'natural organisation of mind, one into which we grow through experience rather than one we achieve through learning'.   (Bruner 1986: 63)

Her reading of Gordon Wells' *The Meaning Makers* (1987) offered her a plausible explanation for another child's difficulty in constructing a sequence of events from memory. Wells suggests that, 'making sense of an experience is to a very great extent being able to construct a plausible story about it' (Wells 1987: 196). She wondered whether the child was unable to construct a story because she could not make sense of her experience or vice versa. She reflected that in either case she would need plenty of talking and reflecting to help her 'through conscious exploration of memory to internalise the meaning of her experiences' (Wendy).

Reflecting on the experience of storytelling

As the students worked with and wrote about the children's experiences of storytelling they were also recording and analysing their own learning. At the end of their four-week school experience they were ready to take stock and reflect on what they had been learning. At one level they had overcome initial misgivings about telling stories and had become experienced practitioners, providing confident models for the children they were working with. At another level, they had produced evidence which enabled them to interrogate the texts that they had been reading as students, to explore and try out hypotheses and develop theories which they were applying to their own experience.

One reflected on her early experience when, 'the story began rather shakily, probably due to my inexperience and slight apprehension at holding 30 children's attention with my voice' (Vicky). As the children began to join in, her confidence increased but she wished that she had been more confident about letting their participation develop and that she had been able to let the children join in and take over a story that they already knew. Another felt that the children had confirmed her belief that stories could be a 'vehicle to understanding yet an end in themselves . . . The intimate and mutually enjoyable nature of storytelling helped to build trusting, positive relationships which formed a secure base from which to explore ideas' (Belinda). Sue recognised that she could now develop aspects of storytelling and would be more confident about bringing the children into the stories by means of song, repetitive phrases and drama. She saw the value of encouraging a wider exchange of stories and was able to suggest ways of doing this: by inviting older children, parents and professional storytellers into the classroom. She ended her account:

I also think that it is important to include stories from different cultures, and where appropriate, in a variety of languages. This would expand the children's experiences of different cultures, promoting and nurturing positive attitudes towards other languages and cultural backgrounds.

Wendy was able to take this further and reflect on its significance,

> by demonstrating that oral storytelling is very important in school we are saying to children that stories have value. By holding in esteem the children's own stories and those of their family or culture we are saying that we hold them and their culture in esteem. Children are very new to the difficult task of reading and writing and for many years after starting school are more likely to be able to express themselves fluently and accurately orally. Giving high esteem to oracy gives children a chance to do well and feel good about themselves long before they have become literate.

By the end of their four-week school experience, students had begun to account for an impressive range of skills and versatility in the repertoire of young children as they created, reshaped and interpreted their experience. They had discovered latent oral narrative skills, both their own and the children's, which they were able to analyse, becoming aware of ways in which a storyteller, in unique ways, is thinking through language. They had also found that narrative was not as easy for children as they had supposed and needed careful planning, intervention and support. Their research and analysis had been supported by their reading. They had found Bruner (1986) and Wells (1987) particularly helpful. Carol Fox's early articles had helped them to recognise ways in which storytelling was helping their pupils to shape experience and develop narrative strategies. They were providing evidence to support Fox's more focused study (1993) which concluded that the model for young children's storytelling is predominantly literary. The pre-school children in her study seemed to use the genre of fantasy stories rather than personal experience since these 'probably lend themselves to a greater degree of elaborating than narrating a real-life experience' (Fox 1993: 97). The students, however, had noticed that their slightly older children were combining both these elements, confidently using the rhetorical devices of the fairy tale and fiction stories that they were hearing in school and combining these with their own real-life experience.

Other influences on the children's developing oracy such as peer interaction on the playground, the shared experience of TV, video and computer games were also becoming evident. By the end of the four-week teaching experience they were all able to draw on the theory they had been reading to analyse the evidence that they had collected and as a group produced a convincing argument for the structured development of children's oral language through storytelling. The importance of narrative in the early development of literacy should not be underestimated:

> Children may find ways into literacy through food labels, model aircraft instructions, or the advertisements lining the motorway. But narrative can be, and for many children is, a particularly inviting, satisfying and empowering path of entry. It provides both a powerful motive for learning to read and much knowledge that will assist the process. This should not be taken to mean that, to young entrants into literacy, narrative is no more than a carrot and a box of useful tools. The sense of semantic reward and the knowledge of what narrative is, as Bruner has shown,

involve vastly complex mental activities (Bruner 1986). Children who engage in the business of building narratives in their heads are extending the arena of their meaning-making to include worlds far wider than the world of the here and now. These worlds are also more ordered, more linguistically self-contained and perhaps more amenable to inspection, than are those created out of the flux of first-hand experience. (Dombey 1992: 1)

Further reading

Grainger, T. (1997) *Traditional Storytelling in the Primary Classroom*. Leamington Spa: Scholastic.

Grugeon, E. and Gardner, P. (2000) *The Art of Storytelling for Teachers and Pupils. Using stories to develop literacy in primary classrooms*. London: David Fulton Publishers.

Note

An earlier version of this chapter was published as 'Becoming Storytellers' by Elizabeth Grugeon in collaboration with Sue Collins, Belinda Louch, Vicky Mansell, Wendy Quince and Jane Templeman in *Early Years: Journal of TACTYC* 10(1) (1989), 10–15.

CHAPTER 4

Developing Children's Oral Skills at Key Stage 2

Prologue

Alex: Mrs Smith, Mrs Smith. I was sick seven times last night and my grandma's gone to Spain.

Hannah: Mrs Smith, Mrs Smith. My hamster's got conjunctibite us.

Stephen: Mrs Smith, Mrs Smith. Have you heard the joke about three pieces of string who went into a pub...My brother told me.

Jamie: Do you believe in all that God stuff, Mrs Smith?

Jessica: Mrs Smith, how do seedless grapes make more seedless grapes if they haven't got any seeds in?

Danny: Mrs Smith, Mrs Smith. Is the steam from coffee different from the steam from tea?

Amrit: Don't you talk them words to me.

David: You f...... b.... You never listen! I hate you! I f...ing I hate you!

Billy: Mrs Smith, Mrs Smith. I know a song from Dublin. My uncle taught it me. I want to sing it you.

Most children of this age love to talk and all primary teachers will know that listening to children's discussions, conversations, stories and anecdotes is one of the most rewarding aspects of our job. The informal moments at school when a little gaggle of children gather round the teacher with all manner of stories, happenings and jokes, competing with each other for her attention have more than just a social value. Through the relationships that develop during these friendly talk times, the children grow more comfortable speaking in more formal learning situations, such as the Literacy Hour. Children will talk to each other and to you, the teacher, about everything under the sun, and they need these opportunities to talk. It is all too easy in today's packed curriculum to think that there is no time for talk. I would argue strongly that today, more than ever, children must be given time to talk about their learning and their experiences

I would like to begin with Billy's story. Billy, Billy, Billy. Billy from Glasgow. Billy who was only with us for four terms, but who, in that time, influenced us all and eventually came to terms with his unwillingness to learn. Billy sang haunting Irish folk songs, perfectly in tune. Billy with his whimsical, cheeky humour and his Gaelic football. Billy with one foot three sizes bigger than the other. We miss him still.

He arrived in Alison's class, Year 5, in the middle of term, troubled, belligerent, barely able to make himself understood, barely able to read or write legibly, vulnerable. What did we make of him? What did he make of us? Gradually, quietly, patiently, at break times, lunch times, before school, after school, he began to make connections. He sought us out one by one. During work time, silence, accompanied by disruptive behaviour. Who could he trust? Who would listen to him?

The first breakthrough came through Jim the caretaker, also from Glasgow, also with a family from Ireland, non-judgemental, kind and quiet. Billy became his shadow and so the silent tours to other classrooms began and his confidence and trust grew. He began talking to us. Each teacher would smile and say 'hello', expecting to be ignored but Billy began smiling at us and looking round our classrooms.

The second breakthrough came with his class teacher. He sang to Alison. The first day back after Easter, just after visiting his father and uncles in Dublin. From that song and Alison's tears came a whole repertoire of songs and from the songs came the stories, his stories – part legend, part folk tale mixed with his own real-life story. From the songs and the stories came other locked-away talents. Brilliant mental maths calculations and Gaelic football. He told Katie all about his skills, she played with him one lunch time and then Billy taught everyone in Year 5 how to play this amazing, fast and dangerous game.

The final breakthrough to the unlocking of Billy's ability to learn came when he sang in sharing assembly. His mother came and 350 staff and children watched him. Alone and unaccompanied. Three songs. One extremely rude we were sure.

What Billy's story illustrates is the power of talking and listening in children's learning. Before his learning could develop, he needed to develop confidence in us, his teachers. He needed to trust us and through listening to him we gained that trust. He became a quiet and modest folk hero throughout the school. He had been listened to and had become a respected member of the school community. By building sensitive relationships with staff and individual teachers in the school, his learning was unlocked and he became a joy to teach and desperate to learn.

It is not just a matter of understanding the power of listening and speaking as a tool for learning for children like Billy. Billy's story was unusual. Most children's stories are less dramatic. We need to appreciate the place and value of speaking and listening in the curriculum for all children at Key Stage 2. The teacher's role embraces the development of speaking and listening not just in English and the Literacy Hour but also across the whole curriculum. This chapter is about organising activities to encourage and support speaking and listening in the primary classroom. It is about stimulating powerful learning. Speaking and listening at Key Stage 2 helps children make sense of their learning and helps them come to terms with feelings and relationships.

There are several voluntary 'tasks' throughout the chapter, which may help you to a wider view of the value of talk at Key Stage 2.

Why is Speaking and Listening such an important element of the curriculum at Key Stage 2?

Pupils talk and listen with confidence in an increasing range of contexts. Their talk is adapted to the purpose: developing ideas thoughtfully, describing events and conveying their opinions clearly. In discussion, they listen carefully, making contributions and asking questions that are responsive to others' ideas and views. They use appropriately some of the features of standard English vocabulary and grammar.

(QCA 1999)

By the end of Year 6, most children will be expected to achieve this level of competency in Speaking and Listening, one of the three attainment targets in the English National Curriculum for England. Many aspects will be taught through the daily Literacy Hour following the NLS framework (DfEE 1998c). Although Speaking and Listening is not identified as a separate strand, it is embedded within the Word, Sentence and Text Level strands. The Literacy Hour cannot be taught effectively without good listening and talking skills.

Overhearing or being part of playground conversations, whether about their school work or about last night's episode of *Neighbours* or *EastEnders*, or the result of a Premier League football match, gives us an insight into the way children make sense of events happening in and outside school. A good moan about a teacher who has had to be angry can help dispel feelings of hurt and frustration.

When children talk about their experiences earnestly, it helps them make critical judgements about personalities, events and relationships. Their discussion and analysis help them resolve conflicts with adults, friends, in games and within their own families. We can and should use this insight into the richness of their oral culture to influence our work in the classroom.

Talking and, of course, listening to others talking, helps children take on new perspectives and adapt, refine or even change previously held beliefs or misconceptions. It guides them towards a clearer understanding of the busy and often complicated lives we lead. As in Billy's case, talk takes children towards a positive view of their own opinions and abilities and leads them to a greater sense of self-esteem and respect for the views of others.

Task 1

Next time you are on playground duty, or have the opportunity to visit a school playground, take the time to listen to the type of talk the children are engaged in, watch their games, listen to their skipping and clapping rhymes. It might prove much more fruitful and certainly more interesting than sorting out fights and arguments! (Remember to take a notebook and a cup of tea with you!)

Comment

You will probably be surprised at how difficult it was to collect this information. Playground talk is not meant to be overheard by adults. We can only guess at the topics being so earnestly discussed 'under the coats'.

In the classroom

Talk in the classroom is crucial to learning. It is where answers to puzzling questions can be found. It is where thoughtful argument and discussion make way for the understanding of new skills and difficult concepts. It is where difficult issues which emerge from the children's literacy work, their maths or science investigations, history or religious education (RE) studies, can be talked through. It is where children listen to and respect the views of each other and where everyone's learning is empowered by talking about what they have learned. It is where children can be supported in raising their own questions about their learning.

Hopefully, by the time most children reach Year 3, or the beginning of Key Stage 2, they will have come to understand the appropriateness of different kinds of talk in different contexts. How and what they talk about will adapt and change, whether they are in the playground, classroom, speaking in sharing assembly, asking questions of a visitor, speaking to the head teacher, talking in twos, larger groups or just to you or the dinner ladies.

Sometimes, out of frustration, disappointment or anger, children may swear and shout at us, taking out on someone they trust and like their pent-up worries and troubles. By giving children the language of argument and persuasion, we can give them the tools to be more effective and articulate at expressing their views in a democratic way.

Speaking and Listening in the curriculum at Key Stage 2

All learning, across the whole curriculum, could be said to begin and end with speaking and listening. It would be almost impossible to introduce any new area of learning or revise an old one without some form of questioning or discussion by the teacher and children. Fortunately, in many areas of the current National Curriculum, talk, discussion, explaining, justifying, describing are all prescribed. Talk in the classroom is protected and being actively encouraged. The whole structure of the Literacy Hour is dependent on good quality teacher and pupil interaction.

The English curriculum, largely taught through the daily Literacy Hour, has a whole section of the Programme of Study devoted entirely to Speaking and Listening, which requires children's abilities to be developed through an integrated literacy programme of Speaking and Listening, Reading and Writing. This includes giving children opportunities that interrelate the Range, Key Skills, and standard English and Language Study themes across the aspects of literacy. The two key words here are 'integrated' and 'interrelated'. It would be impossible to discuss the importance and essential qualities of speaking and listening in isolation.

Task 2

It may be useful to look at some examples of your most recent short-term planning and identify all those opportunities where children's speaking and listening skills were developed and extended.

Comment

You may also like to reflect on how children's talk skills have improved since the advent of the literacy and numeracy strategies. The structure of literacy hours and daily mathematics lessons have enabled children and teachers to engage in a more interactive 'talk' led curriculum. Children need to be able to explain their views, justify choices, methods and decisions.

Children's appreciation of talk as a strategy for learning

Arrangements that help children come to understand and value talk as a strategy for learning include:

- The adoption of a whole-school approach.
- Supportive attitudes in individual teachers, teaching assistants, parents and other children.
- Plentiful opportunities to speak and be listened to.
- Careful planning and organisation of speaking and listening opportunities.

A whole-school approach is the ideal way to help children understand that what they have to say is valued. It should permeate all areas of school life and include relationships with everyone who works in or visits the school. In most schools, Speaking and Listening has equal status in the literacy scheme of work with Reading and Writing. Indeed, it is to be hoped that plenty of discussion of text is the prerequisite of good reading and writing. In weekly planning it is best to ensure several specifically planned speaking and listening opportunities within literacy and other curriculum areas. These could range from children's word explosions for a poetry stimulus, writing and taping a guided tour of a museum room or favourite collection of Ancient Greek or Egyptian artefacts, to a group reporting the results of a science investigation to the rest of the class.

It is significant that as the NLS develops and supportive documents such as *Grammar for Writing* (NLS 2000b) and *Developing Early Writing* (NLS 2001) are being widely used in school, the materials actively promote talk at all stages of the writing process.

Informal talk time

The most important thing a teacher can do to help children appreciate the value of talk is to give children time to talk. Not just curriculum time but time at the beginning and end of the school day. Try to be available for a short time at break and lunch times. There is often a reason why children stay behind to 'tidy up', or why a child is last to put his coat on and collect his lunch box at the end of the day. He may need clarification about something discussed during the day:

Mrs Smith, you know when you said that . . . ?
Is it really true that . . . ?
Can I . . . ?

Many clarifications of the children's learning happen at these informal times. Just as importantly as children talking to you about problems in their learning, they may come, in time, to trust you enough to discuss personal and social issues. This is clearly important for all children but becomes increasingly relevant to the older children at Key Stage 2 as they try to make sense of physical, emotional and psychological changes in themselves.

While discussing triangular numbers with a group of Year 6 children, sitting on the carpet, Alan recounted that he would not be at school on Monday because he was going to his grandfather's funeral. There followed a short discussion between the other children, Alan and his teacher about grandparents, funerals and death. Gary's grandma had died in the summer and he had gone to the funeral and told Alan what it was like. Hayley wished she had been to her aunt's funeral but had chosen not to go. The group then continued laying out counters and looking for patterns in triangular numbers.

Questioning

When teachers speak to children about their work, asking questions is the most commonly used strategy to assess their learning and progress. We can challenge children's thinking if these questions are 'kept open', leading them into other areas of discussion and further questions. Within the NLS, children are encouraged to raise their own questions relating to text in both shared and guided reading. The best way to support children in developing their ability to respond to open or semi-open questions is to encourage them, early in Key Stage 2 or sooner, to prepare their own questions either for the plenary in the Literacy Hour or for other groups to respond to in guided/independent times.

Puzzling questions, primarily used to explore interesting scientific questions, can be a really useful assessment opportunity, encouraging children to think independently or individually in an interesting way and to question their learning. Puzzling questions rarely invite definite answers, more often leading to more puzzling questions. They certainly give children opportunities to discuss their own ideas, particularly in science – 'Why is grass green?' 'Why do we feel pain?' Depending on the context of the questioning, a variety of questioning techniques is to be encouraged.

Giving children time to think before expecting a response

In order to make learning through speaking and listening more effective, teachers need to give children more time to think before expecting a response. We often expect an immediate answer from children, asking 'reliable' children with their hands up. The quality of response will always be better if time is given for individual thought to a whole range of questions. The use of 'talk partners' in both literacy and numeracy can give children an opportunity to think answers through, sometimes with the aid of a 'whiteboard'. By allowing children plenty of time at first, to think their answers through, you might find they need much less time, as their experience deepens, to discuss and arrive at their answer. Many more hands go up and you can actually 'see' the children thinking.

When encouraging less confident speakers, ideas can be shared with a partner or small group; after a little more time, the quieter child will feel able to speak in front of the whole class. Review times during a teaching session help everyone to clarify their thoughts and ideas and frequently spur on those children having difficulty with self-motivation.

Providing the children with an atmosphere of trust in which to talk

Some of the strategies for providing the right atmosphere in which children feel safe to talk have been discussed already in this and preceding chapters. Developing a sensitive and trusting relationship with the children in your class is the most powerful and effective strategy to stimulate talk. However 'quality' talk cannot be left just to 'happen' in the classroom. Certain conditions have to be in place, since structures and a few rules help to create the ideal atmosphere for speaking and listening. The attitudes and responses of children to each other is crucial and no child should ever be laughed at or humiliated for expressing their opinions or points of view.

'Golden Rules for Speaking and Listening' are best initiated by the children but may need a little guidance from the teacher. One class's 'Golden Rule' is that children should try very hard not to interrupt anyone who is already speaking. A 'Golden Rule' for their teacher is to ask her to select a response from a girl and a boy alternately. For older children in Key Stage 2, putting hands up is not always necessary for taking turns. By Year 6, the children have become so used to the 'rules' that shouting out is rare and a different sort of discussion follows. This is called 'open forum' and is used in circle time and discussion of the day's 'puzzling question'. It is surprising how well mannered these precious 'talk' times are and the amount of respect for each other's opinions the children develop.

It is during these times that the teacher should try to hold back and assume that children have something important to say – they nearly always have. Remember, too, you should respond to their questions, as you would to an equal – 10- and 11-year-olds quickly sense if they are being patronised.

When Jamie asked me the God question, I gave the typical teacher's 'sitting-on-the-fence' answer, and immediately knew by the look on his face that I had let him down. He needed more honesty. I did not help him to make sense of his learning. The question, 'Do you believe in all that God stuff?' came when I was sitting with a group of children who were discussing and writing prayers, and he really wanted to know what I thought. I should have given him an 'I wonder', answer.

Task 4

A child in your class asks you if you believe in God. Consider your response. How would you answer the child? Does it matter what sort of response you give? Would it be better put as an 'I wonder' question to the whole class?

Comment

When asked this question, it is important to know your children and be sensitive to their own beliefs.

Creating an environment and atmosphere in your classroom that stimulates Speaking and Listening

With the advent of more discursive and interactive teaching strategies in literacy and numeracy, children are becoming more active listeners and more confident in articulating their learning. However, this does not happen automatically, and the teacher needs to create other 'talk' opportunities and stimuli.

Interactive displays

In common with most primary teachers, I like to have my classroom divided into different areas with lots of interactive displays where children can handle a variety of artefacts. These range from a collection of wooden objects, books and pictures related to science work on materials, to a 'mystery object' relating to a different curriculum area each week. The displays have lots of objects that the children have brought in themselves, and questions relating to them are raised about a specific area of study. I try to change them frequently as the children enjoy fresh displays they can contribute to.

While studying the Victorians in Year 5, we borrowed a collection of 'mystery objects' from the local museum and we learned a great deal together. It was surprising how many questions arose from close examination of a carpet beater!

- Is it a fly swatter?
- Was it to hit naughty children?
- Was it for making jam?

Using role play

The value of role play should not be underestimated or considered important only for early years work. Children of all ages and stages love to dress up or be part of a role-play situation, whether to enhance the understanding of a story book character, or to see a point of view in an argument in literacy, or in other curriculum areas.

When looking to use drama in the Literacy Hour, role play is a simple but effective strategy, particularly if a group of children assume one role or an individual has a team of advisers.

Whole-class — or even school — role-play opportunities can be enjoyed by all and have an imaginative impact on the children's learning. A favourite day in Year 4 is 'Tudor Tuesday'. The children have the opportunity to dress up as pedlars, peasants, archers, famous Tudor characters and to bring a Tudor lunch. A visiting historian comes and leads the children through a variety of authentic workshops. All the Year 4 staff and many parents also lead workshops which include dyeing with natural dyes, dancing a pavane and archery.

During work on the Victorians, using screens and artefacts, we set up replicas of Charles Dickens' and Charlotte Brontë's studies. Here, the children wore shawls, cloaks, bonnets and top hats and wrote with quill pens or fountain pens. Surrounded by aspidistras, old copies of the authors' novels and pictures of Queen Victoria, the children were working in a literary and historical environment. The studies became a favourite retreat for quiet work and reading. The children would 'become' the writers, instinctively changing the way they spoke to each other, very politely and formally, wearing hats! Pioneering work has taken place in Liverpool on the 'Quiet Place' and I have seen caves, tunnels, bird hides all used as a simple 'quiet place' for a different sort of speaking and listening. A place for children to have 'time out' from the normal classroom routines.

In Year 5, while studying St Lucia, we created a very lively Travel Agents in a corner of the classroom, full of travel posters and brochures, a telephone and computer. The children booked many imaginary exotic holidays to the Caribbean. The children could explore routes on maps, work out the cost of flights and holidays and current exchange rates. All this information came from existing geography resources, supported by data from a daily newspaper and a computer data-handling package. A mother of one of the children worked in a local travel agency and came to talk to us about her job, and was bombarded with questions:

Do you go to all the places in your brochures?
What's the most unusual holiday you've booked for anyone?
How much do you earn?

Parents' jobs and experiences can be a wonderful stimulus for talk and discussions about different career possibilities could become a regular feature of school life. Mrs Clarke, another parent, who was born on the island of St Vincent and returned every year for her holiday, came to cook sweet potatoes with the children and tell them about her childhood on the Caribbean island. The discussion and questions that arose from this visit could never have been stimulated by reference books or videos. Her voice and background from another culture was particularly beneficial for the children. They wanted to listen to Mrs Clarke through break time, into the next session and then ask her back.

Useful resources

Time spent on resources that encourage and accommodate talking activities is time well spent. Here are some suggestions:

- a rug or carpeted area for 'on-the-floor' discussions, story and poetry-reading sessions can help to make the talking area comfortable and inviting; the addition of cushions and bean bags can ring the changes for different 'talk' time; care must also be taken as children spend quite a lot of time in literacy and numeracy, sitting for shared text work etc.;
- tape recorders, headphones, microphones and good quality tapes for listening to and recording a whole range of work – science and maths investigations, stories and poems, guided museum tours;
- a quiet area to use the above or for role play – this might only be a small screened-off area in a corner of the classroom;
- carefully presented and displayed fiction, poetry and reference books with open questions and suggested activities for the children to interact with;
- recent newspapers for reading and discussing together (replaced regularly) – these could be in the school library or classroom;
- children's own work on display, read aloud and discussed with the whole class;
- telephones, to be used as part of a role-play situation:

    Nick: 'Hello Das, this is Charlie on the mobile. I'll be late for the meeting';

- hats, shawls, etc., for reading and talking 'in role';
- newspaper photographs and art postcards of people talking – my favourite is a postcard of the 'The Whisper' sculpture by André Wallace which is placed outside Milton Keynes Library – it is of two girls deep in conversation – what are they talking about?

- an 'interesting things we've heard' or 'quote of the week' noticeboard – comments collected by children and teachers – overheard or read in newspapers and magazines;
- an ideas box for circle time discussion topics – these can be anonymous and can cover playground or work-related difficulties – be prepared in the beginning for the occasional 'rude' suggestion – if ignored they quickly stop.

Task 4

Choose a favourite story to read aloud, such as *The Wild Washerwomen* by John Yeoman and Quentin Blake (1985), and try using some props to enhance the storytelling – a basket of washing, an apron or the full washerwoman's or woodcutter's costume. Observe the effects on the children and your own storytelling technique.

Comment

Telling a story to a group or class of children is one of the first activities students are asked to try out in the classroom and it can be a daunting task. It is essential to practise at home, reading aloud to the dog, in front of a mirror or into a tape recorder – preferably dressed up!

Teaching and learning activities for Speaking and Listening

Listed below are several teaching strategies which specifically use speaking and listening as a curriculum focus. None of the activities is exclusive to the teaching of the Literacy Hour or the English Programme of Study. Where appropriate I have made suggestions relating to other curriculum areas. All the suggestions are open to adaptation, variation and development. Many can be found in slightly different forms in related texts and can be recognised as drama, storytelling or poetry-writing conventions. Although these are planned speaking and listening activities, much powerful learning takes place through informal, unplanned, day-to-day, talk and discussion. Specifically organised Speaking and Listening sessions should not be the only opportunities for stimulating talk in the classroom.

1. Teacher-directed discussion/whole-class teaching

Teaching by careful explaining, questioning and informing are some of the most effective teaching strategies. Interactive teacher-led discussion can involve all the children and can stimulate inquiry and a desire to know more. Shared text work in the Literacy Hour relies on whole-class interactive discussion of text, whether the teacher is modelling writing or during supported composition. Sound subject knowledge is helpful in giving the teacher confidence to answer children's probing and demanding questions. The large amount of professional development teachers have received in literacy should raise the quality of talk and understanding in the classroom.

2. Talk partners

This is one of the most successful and easily organised ways of helping children clarify and develop their ideas. It can work with children sitting on the carpet or in groups at tables and can be the preliminary step to working in bigger groups.

Children can simply turn to the person next to them or work with a prearranged partner and talk through their ideas or response to a teacher's question. This is particularly effective as part of whole-class discussion, whether in shared text time or outside the Literacy Hour, and for helping quieter children to feel that their ideas are valued.

Sometimes a time limit can be put on each child's contribution and sometimes the listener can summarise the other person's views to another pair of talk partners. This is an ideal strategy for developing children's listening skills – skills that are every bit as important as the speaking skills. In the heat of the moment children can be so enthusiastic about putting their own ideas forward that they forget to listen to their partner's views.

Working with partners is also an ideal way for children for whom English is an additional language to share ideas in their home language before contributing to a larger group. It can also help their confidence in spoken English if there is no pressure to speak to the whole group.

The role of the teaching assistant both in and outside the Literacy Hour is crucial when working with more reluctant speakers or listeners. She can be a talk partner herself, drawing in reticent children or she can help keep on task those more easily distracted.

This strategy can be used in all curriculum areas but it is particularly useful in the mental and oral starter in the Numeracy Hour. You can use 'sum talk' as a way of explaining how the children have worked out different calculations. With talk partners children first explain their methods to each other, then – the real test of learning and understanding – they are asked to explain their partner's method to a new partner. In this way understanding grows until everyone understands everyone else. Powerful learning!

3. Teaching listening skills

This should be a regular feature of speaking and listening work, even with children at the end of Key Stage 2. Children are encouraged to listen closely to a partner telling them about a particular aspect of learning for three minutes without interruption. They then report what they have heard to another child or group of children. Listening games can also be played in circle time. Children can be encouraged to take notes after watching an educational video rather than during it. You can use a writing framework to help them, along these lines:

- List five things you already know about *The Voyage of Odysseus* before watching the programme.
- Now list five things you have learned about Odysseus's adventures since watching the programme.
- What three things would you now like to find out about Odysseus?

4. Brainstorming

Brainstorming is an effective strategy for initiating discussion, with additional potential as an assessment tool. It enables the teacher to find out more about the children's learning as work progresses. She can assess the children's prior knowledge, what the children are learning and what they have retained about a particular topic. For example 'What do we know already about the Ancient Greeks?' is an opportunity for children to tell us what they know and that last year they went to Crete and visited Knossos and would you like them to bring some photographs in? It is an opportunity for teachers to assess where the gaps are in the children's knowledge and understanding and which aspects of her teaching have worked well.

Brainstorming does not have to be a group activity. It could begin as an individual written activity and then develop to group or whole-class discussion. Individual thinking time can be really beneficial for some children. Others may need the support of sharing ideas with another child or adult. Different techniques and strategies will work at different times for different children and subject areas.

The teacher needs to know her children well before deciding on one particular technique or combination of strategies. Some reluctant talkers become more confident if the teacher sits next to them. This can have the reverse effect on a child who persistently interrupts others. Mixed-ability groups may be daunting for the child with learning difficulties, although sometimes they work very well. Speaking and Listening strategies provide the potential for developing all children's self-confidence and self-esteem. The way children are grouped should be flexible and appropriate to children's needs.

It is often appropriate for the children to write down ideas they have talked about, either as they go along or after preliminary discussion. Try to provide children with a choice of recording materials. Some like to use large sheets of sugar paper and large felt-tipped pens. Others like to use a whiteboard or an exercise book. However, a favourite method of recording is writing ideas onto an overhead projector transparency and presenting bullet points to the rest of the class. These can then be added to as work and learning progresses and finally photocopied for everyone as evidence of the children's emerging ideas. A final 'brainstorm' at the end of the Ancient Greek study should provide evidence that real learning has taken place.

5. Review times: Plenaries, 'pit stops' and 'in-flight checks'

These too may be found in classrooms under a variety of pseudonyms. They are integral and crucial to all good teaching and a successful and helpful Speaking and Listening activity. Whichever way a lesson has been introduced – whether by teacher-led discussion, talk partners, brainstorming, practical demonstration or activity – it is important to sustain the dialogue throughout the follow-up work. Sometimes, through lack of time, evaluation of the children's own learning is rushed or becomes a simple sharing of work. This is a missed opportunity for the children's learning to be valued and for them to explain and justify what they have been learning to the class and their teacher. A final plenary session, planned and focused, is an essential part of the daily Literacy and Numeracy Hours, an opportunity to assess whether the learning objective has been met and where the learning needs refining and developing.

A brief 'pit stop' or 'in-flight check', every so often during an activity can ensure that everyone is on task and understands what is expected of them. It can also help those children who find it difficult to get started. Just hearing someone else's opening paragraph or seeing the beginnings of their gymnastic sequence can help motivate and stimulate ideas. Such reviews can help the teacher pick up on misunderstandings and may help her decide who needs extra support during the lesson. If children know there will be a short review time early on in the lesson, this acts as a motivating force to make early progress.

A much later review time, half an hour or so into the lesson, can be a source of much shared information, thoughts and learning. Each group could be asked to contribute three of their main points or individual children could be asked if they would mind sharing their two best questions, paragraphs or musical compositions.

A final brief review time can take place at the very end of a session where one-sentence summaries of learning outcomes can be shared or one-sentence setting tasks for the next lesson can be reviewed. Plenaries are not just a valuable strategy in literacy and numeracy.

A final review time at the end of the day can reinforce how hard the children have worked and send them home feeling really good about themselves, 'I really deserve to go home and have a rest because I helped plan a really good science investigation' (Charlotte). 'I really deserve to go home and have a rest because I enjoyed my book discussion with Mrs Smith' (Paul).

6. Hot seating

This is very popular with children throughout Key Stage 2. Children of all abilities – not just the more confident speakers – take advantage of its benefits. Individual children are invited to sit in the 'hot seat' and assume the role of a particular book character or unknown person in a photograph or piece of descriptive writing. They then have to answer questions, justify their actions or explain events in their book, photograph or article.

7. Visits, visiting speakers and listeners

The value of educational visits, visiting speakers and visiting listeners has already been referred to earlier in the chapter. They provide children with a focused stimulus to their speaking and listening activities and many have a highly professional approach. One term at a middle school in Milton Keynes yielded the following visits and visitors:

- a residential visit by Year 5 to Shropshire and the Black Country Museum;
- a professional theatre company performing to the whole school;
- the head teacher visiting Year 4 to talk, as part of the children's RE work, about her leadership role;
- a professional artist visiting Year 5 to share her work and discuss the paintings of the pre-Raphaelite Movement;
- a walk to the parish church by children in Year 4 followed by a talk and question session by the parish priest;
- a Book Week hosted by Year 4 and enjoyed by the whole school where parents and teachers visited as 'guest' readers;
- the County School Librarian visited to introduce a book collection of new authors to Year 6 with a follow-up discussion six weeks later;
- a visit to Year 6 by award-winning children's writer, Michael Morpurgo, to talk and answer questions about his writing;
- a visit to the British Museum by Year 6 to study Ancient Greek artefacts, follow-up work to include a written and taped tour guide prepared by pairs of children;
- a teaching assistant visiting the whole school during assembly time to share her expertise in British Sign Language, leading to the establishing of a 'signing' club in school.

This list gives just a sample of activities planned to enhance speaking and listening across the whole curriculum.

8. Reading inside and outside the Literacy Hour

Since the introduction of the Literacy Hour, the systematic teaching of shared and guided reading in both Key Stages is embedded in the daily Literacy Hour. Both these strategies rely on children interacting with text in a meaningful way through discussion and questioning and have provided a clearer focus to their reading development. However, there should still be opportunities for further reading opportunities outside the Literacy Hour.

Poetry reading, non-fiction book reading, reading challenges, oral storytelling, reading conferences and discussions could be regular features of extra reading time in school. A time where children can put into practice all they have learned about reading in the Literacy Hour. The children are encouraged to share their reading experiences with each other and discuss details about their preferences and analysis of text with their teacher, teaching assistant, or reading helper. They might keep a detailed

Reading Log where everyone involved in the child's reading can communicate with each other. This will help link shared and guided reading activities with wider reading at home and in school. The most important contributors to the log are the children themselves.

Reading challenges could take place once a term and the children decide these in discussion with their teacher. Challenges should be adapted and developed according to the age and reading ability of the child. They can be great fun and a real motivation to read in a different way. A selection of challenges may include some of the following:

- Read an easy book backwards from the back page to the front page out loud to a friend.
- Read as many books as you can in a week by the same author.
- Read a book out loud to an older or younger brother or sister every day for a week.
- Read five non-fiction books about something you know nothing about.
- Read a book your mum or dad read when they were your age.
- Bring in three of your favourite books to read to a friend.
- Tell a special story out loud from memory.

Task 5

In discussion with a class or group of children you are working with, find five reading challenges the children would like to meet.

Comment

These challenges can be displayed attractively and it is important that the children keep a record of their challenges and whether they have been able to meet them. They are a real opportunity to help parents remain involved in their child's reading in a lively way, at the same time moving the child to greater reading independence.

A favourite challenge is when the children tell their best story out loud. This need not be a well-known story but could be the child's best 'My Lost Pet' story, or 'My Worst Bike Accident' story or, even better, 'My Getting Lost' story. There can be a real competition to share their stories and a special atmosphere can be created sitting in a circle at the end of the day with the lights dimmed and a candle burning in the middle of the circle.

It is surprising what storytelling skills and talents teachers and student teachers have themselves. A group of undergraduate student teachers, planned and performed, individually and in groups, a stunning array of stories, in costume with many hand-made props to support their stories. The students performed a traditional Anansi story, sung and told in dialect, a retelling in Welsh of *The Little Red Hen*, a hilarious spoof of *Cinderella*, a witty and clever recounting of *The Vicar of Nibbleswicke* by Roald Dahl and several more atmospheric and moving traditional folk tales and legends. The students surprised themselves and each other with the depth of storytelling talent within their group.

9. Circle time

Circle time is one of the single most effective classroom strategies for developing the Speaking and Listening curriculum in Key Stage 2. It is a simple strategy to develop the children's confidence in speaking in front of a large group about topics that are designed to raise their self-awareness and feelings about a whole range of issues. It is a strategy that has grown in popularity in recent years and is now a regular feature of many primary classrooms.

Circle time may be a regular timetabled session in the school curriculum and is often highly valued by the children. It is effective in enhancing the children's behaviour, attitudes to each other, their learning and, above all, their self-esteem. It is an effective strategy for delivering many aspects of the RE syllabus, the Personal, Social and Health Education (PSHE) syllabus and the Speaking and Listening curriculum.

It is easy to organise and can be attempted by teachers at all levels of experience. It is best to begin with getting the children used to talking, reading or sharing in a circle before moving on to a more formal, structured circle time. To begin with, until your own confidence grows, try reading the class reader sitting in a circle, perhaps taking turns to read short extracts or discuss aspects of the text or make observations about an historical artefact. Sitting in a circle gives everyone equal status and you should find those children who are sometimes reluctant to contribute will feel more confident to do so in this setting.

A more formal circle time session might last about 40 minutes and could begin with a 'warm-up' game or activity such as 'Granny's Basket' where each child passes a basket round and chooses an imaginary object to go in the basket, selecting an item beginning with the next letter in the alphabet. For example:

> I have a basket (*child 1*)
> What have you in your basket? (*rest of class*)
> I have an aardvark in my basket (*child 1*)
> I have a basket (*child 2*)
> What have you in your basket? (*rest of class*)
> I have a balloon in my basket (*child 2*)

and so on round the class and through the alphabet.

In playing this game, you might notice a distinct improvement in the imaginative contents of the basket and the vocabulary used by the children to name the chosen object.

'Fruit Salad' is another favourite game where the children are named after a particular fruit. The teacher calls out a child's 'name' and she has to change places with someone who is also a banana, apple, pear or grape. When the teacher says 'Fruit Salad', everyone changes places. This is a good mixing game and although I must have played it hundreds of times no child has ever realised what is happening in the game – it is purely chance who you end up sitting next to!

You could then move on to choose a 'talking object' from a selection in the middle of the room. It can be the privilege of a child who has a birthday during that week to select the object from a variety of soft toys, a clay head, a peacock's feather, a large shell, an alabaster egg or a wooden whale. Children may then only speak when holding the 'talking object'.

You begin by asking each child, in turn, to speak about something lighthearted, such as:

The best thing that has happened to me this week is . . .
The thing I most treasure is . . .
What I'm most looking forward to at the weekend is . . .
The kindest thing I've ever done is . . .

No child is ever forced to speak. If they do not want to comment they simply 'pass' when the 'talking object' reaches them.

You can then move on to discuss more serious issues which a child may have brought to your notice beforehand or put in the suggestion box. Children really appreciate this opportunity to express their worries or concerns. They are quite often about playground or lunch-time issues, but sometimes work worries emerge and can be shared with the whole group who may have suggestions to help. An 'open forum' may follow when other children can make helpful suggestions to improve the situation. For example:

I really don't like it when children swear in the playground.
I am finding it difficult to concentrate on my work table.
I am really missing my grandad.

There are certain circle time 'Golden Rules' which the children stick to as if it was a code of honour. They never mention another child in the circle by name unless it is to say something good about them. Anything discussed in the circle remains confidential and no child should be interrupted when speaking.

The session might close with another light activity such as the 'electric squeeze' where everyone in the circle holds hands and passes round a gentle squeeze.

I have been influenced in my circle time work by the pioneering work of Jenny Mosley, author of several excellent books (see the 'Further reading' section at the end of the chapter) which explain the philosophy behind circle time and make many more excellent suggestions for circle time activities.

Conclusion

Hopefully this chapter will have provided a few well-tried and successful strategies to stimulate quality talk and effective listening in the classroom. These should be seen as a starting point for the student teacher to develop her own strategies for powerful learning at Key Stage 2. Spending time listening to and talking to children will help you towards an understanding of the power of speaking and listening as a tool for learning.

Further reading

Goodwin, P. (2001) *The Articulate Classroom*. London: David Fulton Publishers.

Mosley, J. (1993) *Turn Your School Round*. Cambridge: Learning Development Aids (LDA).

Mosley, J. (1996) *Quality Circle Time*. Cambridge: Learning Development Aids (LDA).

Mosley, J. (2000) *More Quality Circle Time*. Cambridge: Learning Development Aids (LDA).

CHAPTER 5

Developing Exploratory Talk

Introduction

Computers are designed for individual use, but children in primary classrooms very often work at the computer in a group. This is partly because of the scarcity of computers in schools, and partly because teachers believe that children in groups can support one another by talking about their work. It is often difficult for teachers to supervise computer groups directly, and so groups must be self-sufficient, with the support of high motivation generated by the computer. In these circumstances, it is important that the talk that goes on is productive, in terms of engaging the group through the software, and educationally useful in its content and scope.

Can we be sure that children's talk at the computer will be educationally useful? Can we say what 'educationally useful' is – what sort of talk we expect ? And if so, can we encourage the most useful types of talk?

Researchers based at The Open University worked with teachers to observe children talking together at the computer in primary schools. Their aim was to listen to children using a variety of software, and to look for patterns in their interaction which would answer the fundamental question: what sort of talk goes on? This chapter starts by looking at some examples of talk around computers, goes on to describe aspects of the spoken language of interest to teacher, and ends with issues of classroom organisation.

Children talking

Below are three transcripts of groups of children talking together (data taken from the *Spoken Language and New Technology* or *SLANT* project). There are some obvious dissimilarities: for example, the children are not using the same software and Transcript 2 records the talk of two girls, rather than a mixed group. But each of the groups was given the same direction by their teacher – to work together on the task. As you read through each of the extracts, consider the following questions:

(a) Do any of the transcripts contain the sort of talk you, as a teacher, would expect to be taking place while children are working in school?

(b) Are the children functioning as a group? That is, are they collaborating with one another, or do they seem to be working individually?

(c) Are the children considering one another's ideas carefully?

(d) Do the children request information from one another?

(e) Does anyone give a reason for what they say?

(f) Which transcript contains talk of a kind that you think is educationally most valuable? Can you say why?

Transcript 1: Taking turns

Three children – Jade, Lucy and Micky – have been asked to work together to complete some non-verbal reasoning tests which were presented to them as 'puzzles'. They have to choose which one of eight tiles will match a given background pattern.

Micky:	See, I told you!
Lucy:	Shut up, Micky!
Micky:	People will think –
Lucy:	Stop showing off!
Jade:	I know what these are.
Micky:	One, two, three. Now it's my turn.
Lucy:	No, it's not your turn! It was your turn just a minute ago!
Jade:	It's number eight.
Lucy:	Now it's your turn, Jade.
Jade:	Number eight and number seven.
Micky:	Now it's my turn. Don't tell me.
Jade:	That one, Micky.
Micky:	Big, middle, and small.
Lucy:	It's your turn – no, it's my turn. It's that one.
Micky:	That one.
Lucy:	No, that one's already been on.
Micky:	Where, where, where, where!
Lucy:	Stop it! Shut up, Micky!
Jade:	There's loads that haven't been on. There's loads that haven't been on!
Lucy:	Micky, it isn't your turn.
Jade:	It's my turn, actually.

Transcript 2: Does that look better?

Two children, Angela and Bridget, have been asked to work together to compile a page for the class newspaper. They have done some research in the library, and are now sorting out the format of the information on the screen.

Bridget:	Does that look better?
Angela:	OK.
Bridget:	Down, yes.

Angela:	OK, OK.
Bridget:	Does that look alright or too small?
Angela:	OK. What happened to my...it's supposed to be on the first page/second page as well.
Angela:	How does that sound? (*reads quote*)
Bridget:	Yes that sounds good, we have to do something, because we've done animal testing on this, we've got to do something a bit...it's a bit heavy.
Angela:	Yes I know. I'm not going to put it on page three.
Bridget:	Four.
Angela:	I said I'm not going to put it on page three.
Bridget:	Yes I know.
Angela:	...we'll have to scatter a few jokes on this page.
Bridget:	Yes and some of the names quiz.

Transcript 3: Ain't worth it, is it?

Three children – Gavin, Sara and Tammy – have been asked to work together to agree on a suitable outcome for a story which has a moral dimension. The story is about Kate, whose friend Robert has told her that he stole a box of chocolates from a shop, to give to his mother who is ill. Kate has promised not to tell anyone.

Gavin:	(*reads*) Kate was worried. Should she tell her parents or not. Here are some of her thoughts. Stealing is wrong. I promised not to tell anyone. Robert is my friend, if I tell he will get into trouble. Robert is kind. He stole the chocolates for his sick mother. Talk together and decide what Kate should do. Then click on one of these buttons. Does not tell her parents or tells her parents. (*reading ends*) Right we've got to talk about it. (*Tammy looks at Sara*)
Tammy:	What do you think?
Sara:	What do you think?
Gavin:	I think even though he is her friend then, um, she shouldn't tell of him because, em, well she should tell of him, em, because was, was, if he's stealing it it's not worth having a friend that steals is it?
Tammy:	No.
Sara:	Why? I don't agree.
Tammy:	We said why. I think that one as well do you? (*Tammy points to the screen and looks at Sara*)
Gavin:	I think she should tell her parents. Do you?
Tammy:	I think I'm – I think even though he is her friend, because he's stealing she should still tell her parents, and her parents might give her the money and she, she might be able to go to the shop and give them the money.

Sara:	I think um –
Gavin:	– but then she's paying for the thing he stole, so I think he should get the money anyway. He should have his –
Sara:	I think that he should go and tell his mother.
Gavin:	– own money Mum.
Tammy:	– even though she has promised.
Sara:	Because he's, well you shouldn't break a promise really should you?
Gavin:	What's it worth having a friend if he's going to steal?
Tammy:	If he steals. If you know he's stolen if she don't tell her parents then he will be getting away with it.
Gavin:	It's not worth having a friend that steals is it? *(Three-second pause)*
Sara:	OK then.
Tammy:	Ain't worth it is it?
Sara:	Tells her parents. *(Sarah clicks mouse)*
Gavin:	Yeah go on.
Tammy:	*(reads)* Robert stole a box of
Gavin:	A box of chocolates from Mrs Cook's shop.

Comment

The way the children have interpreted the teacher's instruction (to work together) differs widely.

Transcript 1: Taking turns

In this group, the children are in competition with one another. Little information is shared, and much of the talk is to do with the impossible task of making the turn-taking 'fair'. Each is trying to sort things out in their own way, but their styles of doing so conflict, and the children blame one another for this.

Transcript 2: Does that look better?

In this short extract from a much longer tape containing largely the same sort of talk, the children are working together agreeably. They accept one another's ideas without querying them. It is the sort of talk that goes on between friends who have decided to help one another. The page is being compiled steadily by the girls, with no critical appraisal of its quality or design.

Transcript 3: Ain't worth it, is it?

In this group, the children engage with one another in a serious discussion. They question one another's ideas, and ask one another for reasons to justify assertions they make. This is done in a spirit of open enquiry, and all voices are heard. Opinions are respected. Eventually they are able to reach a decision to which they have all contributed.

Types of talk at the computer

Evidently, very different kinds of talk were taking place between children working together at computers. Three particularly distinctive categories could be identified.

1. Disputational talk

This is characterised by disagreement and individualised turn-taking. There are few attempts to share knowledge or to offer suggestions. There are short exchanges which consist of assertions and challenges or counter-assertions. The participants are in competition with one another, and each seems to have strong, but unstated, ideas about what constitutes winning. Transcript 1 is a clear example of disputational talk.

2. Cumulative talk

The speakers build positively but uncritically on what the other has said. This sort of talk is characterised by repetitions, confirmations and elaborations, as in Transcript 2.

3. Exploratory talk

The group engages critically but constructively with each other's ideas and statements or suggestions are offered for joint consideration. These may be challenged, but justifications are expected and given consideration. Alternatives are offered and reasons requested, with knowledge being shared, and reasoning more evident in the talk. Progress emerges from the eventual joint agreements that are reached, and any decisions 'belong' to the entire group, as in Transcript 3.

Further discussion about these varieties of talk may be found in Mercer (1995).

Teachers specify 'exploratory talk' as the sort of talk that they would particularly want to encourage between children working in groups, at the computer or during any other task. However, disappointingly little exploratory talk took place in the classrooms observed. The computer tasks were motivating and the children worked steadily, but their talk was largely to do with managing the issues of turn-taking, with unquestioning agreement or disagreement, or with reaffirming their own social position in the class. The children did not seem to have understood that that they might use talk as a tool for exploring one another's ideas, and to reason together.

The value of exploratory talk

What is it about exploratory talk that makes it such an important sort of interaction? And if a teacher hopes or aims to encourage exploratory talk between children in her class, how can she help them to achieve this?

First, let us look at the other two types of talk described above. Cumulative talk is appropriate in many circumstances in classrooms, where uncritical agreement is all that is required to complete a task. Children doing a jigsaw, or collaborating to present a joint piece of work, would do well if they talked this way. Its strength is that it draws on the friendship and mutual trust of its participants, who are 'easily pleased' with one another, and agree to each other's ideas without examining either the idea or their own response to it. However, the very *strength* of cumulative talk is its weakness when it comes to the crucial stages of problem solving or decision making where agreement is reached without reasons being properly considered. There is no evidence of rational thinking in cumulative talk. That is not to say that the children are acting irrationally, but that they are not making their reasons explicit to one another. If asked, they might well be able to articulate their reasons for assertions and suggestions, but in cumulative talk they make no attempt to do so, and are not encouraged to do so by their work mates. The talk, and the engagement with the task, is superficial.

You might think about the effect that working with a partner can have on the child as an individual. Talking with a partner is an opportunity to put half-formed ideas into words. Having to say what you mean – thinking aloud – is a way of making your thoughts clear to yourself: and having to say things to a partner is a way of developing a shared understanding of ideas. If your partner is prepared to accept your initial suggestion, without you having to justify or defend it, you have no stimulus to engage critically with your own thoughts. Also, you have no alternative suggestions to produce the creative friction from which new ideas arise. This *interthinking* – the joint engagement with one another's ideas to think aloud together, solve problems or make mutual meaning – is an invaluable use of spoken language (Mercer 2000).

Rationality is also not apparent in disputational talk. Children challenge one another's knowledge without offering reasons, and disagree with one another's ideas without offering alternatives. They deny the ideas that are offered, and in doing so appear to deny that the child offering a suggestion has any right to do so, or to have any idea worthy of consideration. Looking back to Transcript 1, see how often Micky made suggestions that were not accepted. If he had offered reasons for his suggestions, or if he had been given reasons for the rejection of his ideas, then the discussion might have helped him to understand why his ideas were treated this way – he might have learned something. And if all three children had considered their own reasoning, their talk together would have had a purpose more crucial to the development of their thinking than that of simply trying to do the puzzles.

Exploratory talk allows a reasoned exchange of ideas and opinions. This sort of talk is likely to be of great value to the children educationally, because it means that they are using language to think rationally, and to consider and evaluate each other's ideas in a cooperative way. They can build up shared knowledge and shared understandings, as they engage in opportunities to collaborate as equals. Collaborative talk of this kind provides a supportive context for thinking aloud, and thinking aloud is crucial if children are to formulate their thoughts and ideas. It also represents the kind of rational, considered debate at the heart of 'educated' activities such as science, law and politics. Engaging in interthinking through rational discussion with other people is likely to help children develop clearer ways of thinking to support their development as an individual.

Encouraging exploratory talk

Exploratory talk is difficult enough for adults to achieve and it cannot be assumed to 'come naturally' to children. Some children in primary classrooms may be familiar with exploratory talk from their prior experience in and out of school. They may be capable of using this as a model for their talk with their peers. Other children who have relatively little experience or awareness of exploratory talk may be completely unfamiliar with using rational discussion as a means of resolving conflicting views or negotiating a joint solution to a problem. Unlike reading, writing, science and mathematics, talk is learned informally and is in constant use; its very familiarity may make it 'invisible' as a tool for learning. It may not occur to children that the way they talk to other people makes a difference to what they achieve. They may need to be guided into understanding how different ways of talking together can produce different outcomes in their work, and in their life beyond the classroom.

Simply grouping children to work together at a computer will not necessarily help them to develop talking skills. Research such as that undertaken by Bennett and Dunne (1992), has shown that children often don't know what is expected of them in collaborative work, and they need direction on this from their teachers. The sleeve notes with educational software may state that 'encouraging discussion' is one of its aims, but unless children know what we expect about the quality of their discussion, they may gain little of educational value from the talk or the activity. The computer can provide an excellent environment for practising exploratory talk, once this way of talking has been introduced to the children.

Teaching ground rules for talk

Children who are expected to work together in groups need to be taught ho   ۱ʟ to one another. They need talk skills which will enable them to get the best c own thinking and that of all the other members of their group. Th understand and share the aims for their talk, with the teacher and with

Before they can use the computer to practise discussion skills, they need to be taught what the elements of those skills are. They must understand that if all the group can agree on a set of rules, 'Ground Rules for Talk', then talk can proceed in a way which will make the whole group, and its individuals, more effective.

The next part of this chapter develops a way of encouraging children to become more aware of their talk, and of helping them to compile a set of ground rules to ensure that the high quality of talk at the computer is as much the aim of the children as it is of the teacher. Ground rules which can enable a group to discuss things with one another may not be entirely obvious to children. They have to be disentangled from other rules for talk that they will have learned, or at least heard of. Asked for their ideas about rules for talk, children may suggest:

> Only speak when you are spoken to.
> Be quiet in the library.
> Don't interrupt an adult.
> Don't use bad language.
> Don't shout in the classroom.

Useful as these may be, they are not relevant to engaging in interthinking. Ground rules for discussion are to do with collaboration, and have embedded in them the purpose of group talk. Such rules can help children interacting with software to focus on its content rather than the interface. Such work is not always easy, and with no rules to coordinate the group, talk together may be of a variety more suited to the playground than the classroom.

Teaching talk: some practical points

Grouping children to enable exploratory talk

The ways teachers group children is quite a subtle process. A teacher must take into consideration such factors as time constraints, the general knowledge and ability of the children, their gender, sociability or otherwise, computer literacy, and imaginative powers as well as their friendship groups, personalities, and listening and talking skills. There are more mundane considerations such as who is present or absent in class on any particular day, who is least behind with other class work, and the exacting demands of the classmates for 'fairness' in turn-taking at the computer. Figure 5.1 outlines some factors that have to be taken into account when grouping children.

Despite careful composition of the groups some or all of the following problems may arise:

1. The children may understand what is required by the program, but they do not understand the intended purpose of their talk together. They do not know how to negotiate with one another, and using the computer will not teach them this directly.

2. Self-appointed group leaders emerge and impose an inappropriate style of working on the group. Those with home computers are proficient with the keyboard and used to playing games where speed is more valuable than talk or cooperation. Keen to show their skill, they dominate the group.

3. Friends tend to agree with one another on principle, and less confident children make no contribution at all, to avoid being held responsible later on. Difficulties with the program and each other cause some children to abandon the group altogether, saying they are 'going back to work'.

4. The talk is of a casual or social nature. Since the computer group is not overtly supervised by the teacher, the children engage in their constant testing and re-establishment of the class 'pecking order', and this process dominates the talk.

5. Boys and girls act out stereotypical gender roles, which usually means that boys dominate the proceedings: I will return to this later in the chapter.

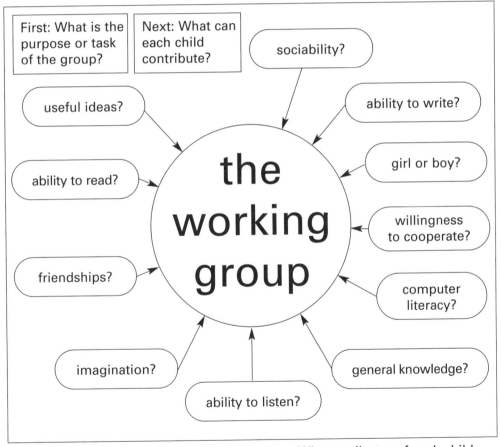

Figure 5.1 Grouping children to work together: What attributes of each child could be considered?

The computer as a problem

Paradoxically, one problem with computers arises from their popularity. Both children and teachers seem to like computers, for reasons not always strictly connected with their educational value. They allow children to work at their own pace, and to produce clear copy and impressive artwork. They can be fun, introducing an element of play into learning, and bringing the appeal that expensive and highly technical machines seem to have for many people. Things can go wrong, with hours of effort lost in moments, but they remain popular, and their increasing prevalence makes it imperative that schoolchildren learn how to use them. But unless children's work on a computer-based activity is well organised, it may achieve little of educational value.

The choice of software depends on what is available in school to fit in with the class topic, or to match individual children's needs. As a teacher-researcher I (Lyn Dawes) based some activities on a program called BRANCH, which provides a framework for constructing keys by classifying objects in a hierarchical way. I felt that this software would encourage discussion in small groups working together. The class were using this to construct a key which others could use to identify given articles. The children were familiar with the program, having used it to sort toys and models and went on to use it to sort rocks for their topic study. Completing a key involved looking carefully at the rocks and thinking of a question with a yes/no answer which would distinguish them from one another. I had thought that their talk together would be to do with the observable and measurable features of the rocks, with some debate about which suggested question would be most sensible. This had been the focus of preliminary class discussion.

However, the videotaped evidence showed that this preparation had apparently had little effect on the quality of the children's talk. The children lacked discussion skills, and this hampered their work with BRANCH and with other software involving problem solving, decision making or collaborative writing. The finding that children who were asked to work together as a group did not seem to understand clearly enough what teachers meant by 'collaboration' or 'discussion' fitted with those of others (Bennett and Dunne 1992; Edwards and Mercer 1987; Mercer 1995; Wegerif and Scrimshaw 1997). The children were not misbehaving or 'off task' – just unaware that they were expected to engage in more effective ways of interacting. They were unclear about the 'ground rules'. They had not understood the expectations for their talk because I had not made this aspect of the work explicit to them.

Ground rules for exploratory talk

These are some ground rules for facilitating and generating exploratory talk:

- the group takes responsibility for decisions
- all relevant information is shared

- the group seeks to reach agreement
- reasons are expected
- challenges are accepted
- alternatives are discussed before a decision is taken
- all in the group are encouraged to speak by other group members.

This set of rules was incorporated into aims for lessons and used to generate a number of lesson plans designed to encourage discussion. Using these lesson plans I taught a new topic to my class at the beginning of the new school year – 'Talking Lessons'. One special aspect of these lessons was that their aims were primarily to do with talking and were made explicit to the children. (The lesson plans for the Talking Lessons described here can be found in Dawes *et al.* (2000) or at http://www.thinkingtogether.org.uk.)

Talking Lessons

At the point that the Talking Lessons began, it appeared that some of the children in my class could talk confidently, but not listen carefully to others. Others shied away from engaging one another in protracted talk, as if they found any difference of opinion very worrying, and were unable to distinguish a sensible discussion from a more threatening argument. Some used a way of being generally agreeable, or disagreeable, to remain uninvolved, while others simply dictated or asked for orders.

To work more effectively as a group, the children needed to be taught how to talk to one another in a way that was both impersonal and intimate. It was impersonal because once they had mastered it they could talk like that to anyone, and intimate because it would establish mutual trust for the sharing of ideas, and give them access to one another's thoughts. Over a whole term, in special groups, the class took talking lessons, most of them not involving the computer. Before each lesson, I explained to the children that the idea was to develop their awareness of talk, and help them work together better. I told them exactly what my aim was for their talk, and checked that they understood what I meant and agreed to try it. They undertook various activities designed to encourage them to exchange opinions, describe things and events to one another, listen to and relate facts and stories, and state and defend the reasons behind their suggestions.

Ground rules for talk: children's version

Below are the ground rules for talk generated by the children during the Talking Lessons programme. It is interesting to compare them with the 'adult' version in the previous section. All the crucial elements are here, but translated into manageable and sensible 'rules' by the children. The children liked the rules because they had suggested them, decided which were essential, and agreed to them, and they understood that such rules would help them work more productively with a group. They tried to bear them in mind in their work together, and they referred to a display poster of the rules if they felt that someone needed to be reminded.

Class 5D agree that:

1. everyone should have a chance to talk
2. everyone's ideas should be carefully considered
3. each member of the group should be asked
   – what do you think?
   – why do you think that?
4. we will look and listen to the person talking
5. after discussion, we will agree on an idea before we enter it in to the computer.

The effect of the Talking Lessons

The class agreed to use the rules when it was their turn to work with the computer. They reminded themselves and each other of the rules before they began work. By the end of the talk topic, a marked improvement in the quality of the children's talk at the computer was evident. This was confirmed by analysis of videotapes of the children talking. After the intervention, more examples of exploratory talk were evident in the video recordings, and more time was spent on talk before decisions were made. Reasoning was evident in the talk.

As in any mixed-ability class, some of the children had developed their discussion skills quickly, while others found it hard to listen, hard to talk, or hard to think of reasons for their assertions. They would need a little longer, but their classmates could remind and coach them. However, the entire class had a heightened awareness of talk as a tool for working together and a clearer idea what they might do with talk. The video evidence showed that many of the children had learned how to negotiate their ideas, and that they were able to consult the other members of the group and give proper attention to their views. They could ask one another for opinions, and make their own reasoning explicit in their talk. The members of the group had a joint understanding of the importance of their talk and had learned some skills which would support one another's attempts to discuss ideas and reach a joint conclusion. The children discussing Kate's Promise, 'Ain't worth it, is it?' (Transcript 3) were recorded after a course of Talking Lessons.

The children worked together at the computer more effectively once they had learned how to talk to one another in this way. The computers provided an extremely useful and motivating means of practising exploratory talk, once it had been initiated by the talk programme. Many children are adept at discussion and reasoning but others are not, and children who are isolated in their ability to reason may quickly resort to a less taxing disputational style, even though it is obviously more frustrating. Once a class, or most of a class, has exploratory talk in its repertoire, the individuals can work with each other, because the 'rules' are clear and have been agreed in advance.

The Talking Lessons had another interesting outcome. The children who had undertaken the programme also showed an increased ability to solve reasoning problems on their own, which the researchers associated with the shift towards critical questioning in their use of spoken language. That is, they seemed to have 'internalised' the kind of reasoning that they had been doing in their groups. Because they had been required to reason aloud, they could now use this skill individually to reason when faced with a decision.

Many of my class obviously found it very useful to be able to challenge another group member in a way that would not provoke conflict. Others, as you would predict, never quite got the hang of it, and would get frustrated by what they felt was too much sitting around talking. They would try to go back to putting their foot down in one way or another. Exploratory talk was, after all, an aim, not a prescription. It would not be reasonable to expect children to be fluent at any unfamiliar skill without plenty of opportunities to practise. The computer provided just some of these opportunities. However when the class moved to their next teacher for the new school year, she told me that as a class she found them unusually reasonable with one another when it came to sorting out classroom conflicts.

I no longer expect children to talk to one another effectively at the computer unless I have taught them how to do so. Some computer programs, such as spelling games, tables practice or word processing, do not require group collaboration. But I teach the Talking Lessons first anyway, because the rationality required by exploratory talk is a vital tool that the child can use in all areas of the curriculum.

Talk, reasoning and computers

Further classroom research has shown that giving children the opportunity to engage with one another in exploratory talk may help them to reason better with themselves, as well as with others. Children who understand and can use collaborative ground rules for talk can use spoken language more effectively as a tool for learning. (Wegerif *et al.* 1997). For example, when children's individual and group scores on non-verbal reasoning tests are carried out before and after a Talking Lessons programme the four main findings are:

1. using exploratory talks helps groups of children to work more effectively together;
2. the Talking Lessons programme increased the amount of exploratory talk children used when working together;
3. children who had undertaken Talking Lessons improved their individual results on reasoning tests;

4. children who can engage in interthinking, with the structure of their agreed ground rules for talk, are practising talk-based thinking skills which they can then use when solving problems on their own.

Developing your critical awareness of the quality of talk

This chapter has described how some of the talk that goes on around computers can be understood, and has suggested one sort of intervention that has been found to produce a measurable change in the quality of children's talk. In this section, there are some examples of talk around the computer for you to consider, with brief notes about their context, and comments for you to compare with your own ideas.

Some children may encourage one another to think of the time they spend at the computer as some sort of play time. They may amuse themselves by typing 'naughty' words or by thinking of ways to make the work more like a game. Their talk is as it would be when using a computer at home, and is to do with amusing each other and reconfirming friendship and shared values. Of course this sort of talk is essential in its usual setting, but bringing it into the classroom is an effect that computers can create. Because the computer 'allows' it children may, for example, include cartoon-type violence in stories. In the following extract, Stephen and Mark are using a program in which they can select objects and people from a bank of pictures, and write a story for their choice of illustration. Before this conversation occurs, they have already created a girl character who crashes her boat into some rocks and drowns. The 'dead body' remains on the screen for some time. Their (boy) character moves into a cave as Stephen and Mark continue writing together.

While you read through the talk, consider these points:

- Are the boys 'on task'?
- Does this talk fall into any of the categories described as cumulative, disputational, or exploratory (remembering of course that there is much talk that cannot be categorised in this way)?
- Do you think the boys are enjoying writing their story?
- If you think they are, can you think why?
- If you think they are not, can you think why?

Transcript 4: Skeleton

S: You get to a cave and wander in
M: Yeah
M: (*reads*) As you are not the cleverest person in the world (*laughs*)
S: (*still typing*) You get lost. You ask the goblin (*points to screen*) for help . . . yeah?
M: Yeah. But then his friend jumps on you and kills you . . . and that could be the end of you

S: Yeah

M: And then we have to go the other way – yes – no – and you chop his head off or something

S: You ask the (*typing in*) goblin for help...and while your back is turned the skeleton jumps on top of you and kills you

M: The skeleton jumps on top of you but you knock him off

S: Yes

M: You knock him off

S: His body is scattered over a large area

M: But he pulls himself together and goes to sleep on the rock

S: (*typing*) He sneaks up behind you

M: and you

S: I think it would have been best if we had seen what the (proper) one was (*reads*) the skeleton sneaks up behind you (*typing*) It leaps on top of you...but you manage (*types* 'to knock it off and')

M: Has that page got enough? Knocks it off...oh

S: (*typing*) Bones fly everywhere

M: Fly everywhere

S: (*inaudible*)

M: Is that how you spell 'every'?

S: Alright...alright (*corrects spelling by inserting a second 'e'*)

M: I was just wondering. It looked a bit weird

S: Knock it off and bones fly everywhere

M: And then it picks itself up and pulls itself together

Comment

The boys are completely engaged in their writing task. Much of the talk is cumulative. This sort of collaborative talk enables both of them to contribute to a joint outcome; they can rely on their partner to agree with their ideas, with little reflection. They are enjoying making up what is a sort of mild horror story with content that is slightly subversive! This collusion is more likely to occur between friends, and while it is perfectly possible for boys and girls to be friends, most children choose a 'best friend' who is the same sex as themselves. Pairs of friends of either sex will tend to engage in cumulative talk. This is pleasant for them and can result in good finished work for some sorts of tasks. But if the task set by the teacher requires problem solving, friends working together might not be the most productive grouping. And if the aim for the talk is that the children elicit reasons and counter-reasons, the same is true.

In the following extract, Hannah and Lisa, aged nine, are using the art package 'Paintspa'. They are drawing a house in a field by a river, to go with a story that the class has been putting together. As you read through the transcript, try to think about the following questions:

- What do you think each child is aiming to achieve?
- Do their aims coincide?
- Do you feel that these two girls are friends, in the way that Angela and Bridget are in the transcript 'Does that look better?'?
- Are the children 'on task'?
- Do you think they will leave the computer feeling content with their work together, and satisfied that it reflects the effort they have put into it?

Transcript 5: Rubbing out

Hannah:	I love doing rubbing it out. Do you?
Lisa:	Hang on
Lisa:	Oh yeah. I don't need to. I just need to take a square
Hannah:	a square
Lisa:	Why have we come down? (*inaudible*) Hannah it's not working. Now. Where are you?
Hannah:	Better (*inaudible*)
Lisa:	Hey I've found it and you pushed it away. Plonker. Eh, eh, oops. (*inaudible*) When we . . . that's better, ain't it? Let's go along a bit more yeah? Along a bit more
Hannah:	No, no, no that's it. It's that
Lisa:	(*inaudible*)
Hannah:	Across now. Across. Stop. Across. Stop. Down
Lisa:	(It says) undo. It doesn't matter about that bit. So we just need to go down
Hannah:	Go down. Let me do this bit
Lisa:	No, I want to do it
Hannah:	Ah, ah. Down. Across. Right now let me do this one
Lisa:	Oh what. We want to do the river, don't we? We want to do the river now
Hannah:	Not yet. Not yet
Lisa:	I want to do the river. I want to do the river first
Hannah:	You can't. We ain't done the boat
Lisa:	I'm doing the river
Hannah:	Not on there. The river's going to be that . . . polluted river
Lisa:	I know. I've got to go all the way back to that thing just there and then we've got to go up, haven't we?
Hannah:	Yeah. No we've got to go down and across a bit
Lisa:	Um
Hannah:	Across. Across more
Lisa:	Ohh
Hannah:	There not much more across. Oh come on
Lisa:	We've got to have one of these each, ain't we

Hannah: You want to do it now? Would you like to swing on a star (singing) bum bum bum carry moon beams swing on a star um um um. Would you like to swing on a star ow ow ow

Lisa: I like these (colours)

Comment

Hannah and Lisa have been asked to work together on a picture. But they cannot agree on anything that appears (or disappears) because they have not shared their conception of the finished product with one another, and are not doing so as they go along. It is interesting how disputational talk like this can be part of a creative process, in that a finished product results; but the creation entails what appears to be a high level of frustration. It appears that neither of the children will feel ownership or pride in the finished result, since it is not what either of them wants separately, and they are not collaborating in a way that would make it a satisfying joint enterprise. They do not negotiate ideas or ask one another for reasons. The role of the computer in this scenario is overtly to provide the means of constructing a picture, and covertly to be a third party, reflecting the wishes of whoever had hold of the mouse last.

The children will no doubt have work to show but they will not have extended their talk repertoire or practised special and useful talk skills. This is fine, as long as the teacher is aware that it is the case. If the children are fiddling around at break time, trying to see how the program works, this sort of disputational talk might be acceptable. But in the context of a school day, in which a 'turn' on the computer is still something of a privilege, it is perhaps a waste of the children's time. And they certainly display signs of being slightly disengaged by the end of this session. But they have not given up. This persistent effort in the face of continual failure to master the program, and constant unhelpfulness from their partner, is a tribute to the motivating power of the computer, and of course to the determination of the individuals. If their individual commitment had been directed into a group effort, and their talk disciplined towards negotiation, they might have succeeded better.

Most children do their best to collaborate with their partner most of the time, but they may not know how to negotiate with another child whose agenda for the shared activity is very different from their own. The social positions held by boys and girls are naturally extremely important to them, and their interactions inevitably contain an element of awareness of this. Effective talk can help individual children to truly collaborate, that is to express their own ideas lucidly and at the same time find out what their work mates are really thinking about the task in hand. The advantage of teaching about talk, teaching children how to question one another, negotiate ideas, share information, and attempt to reach a reasoned agreement, is that the ground rules underlying the ensuing discussion help to avoid the effects of gender conditioning, friendship groups, and other social brick walls that prevent children learning.

More about talk between girls, boys and friends

Equality between girls and boys is a fundamental aim of the class teacher. Grouping children to work together at the computer requires an awareness of gender issues, and a determination to counteract imbalances. Research evidence shows that boys in class tend to be more assertive than girls, to call out more often, and to occupy more space.

Joan Swann, in *Girls, Boys and Language* (1992), discusses this issue more thoroughly. Classroom investigation shows that boys tend to monopolise resources, and teachers are likely to give them more attention. Girls and boys contribute differently to classroom talk. Computers are a particular area of concern, because in spite of the prevalence of women using computers in the workplace, they may still retain their image as 'boy's toys'. Boys make greater use of computers out of school than girls, and even those who don't are prepared to be more confident about using school computers. Some boys may therefore unwittingly dominate technological resources in various ways, for example by simply positioning themselves in front of the keyboard and screen or taking control of the mouse. Some boys are so keen on computers that they perceive equality as unfairness to themselves, and say so. There are of course many vociferous and assertive girls, and many girls who are drawn towards computers, but teachers have found that it is often boys who behave as if they 'own' technology, and this can cause problems for groups.

It isn't easy to tackle this problem since it is part of a much larger social issue. However, it's important to be aware of the different ways that boys and girls may approach group work at the computer, and the problems that may arise because of the behaviour they bring to the task. Encouraging the children to become aware of their own perceptions of one another may help as strategy for discouraging prejudice which possibly has its origins in thoughtlessness.

Conclusion

If using discussion skills is one of the aims of grouping children to work together at a computer, then, first, the children must be made aware of this, and, secondly, they must be explicitly provided with the skills they will need to do what the teacher expects of them. Providing Talking Lessons is one way to introduce such skills, with the class creating and agreeing to a set of ground rules for talk which will provide a basis for all discussion. Teachers play a crucial role in raising children's awareness of how to use talk effectively.

As the educational researcher Peter Scrimshaw (1993: 108) has put it:

Computer use is a social practice in which the ways in which the actors interpret and approach their tasks are as influential as the characteristics of the hardware and software itself. One important and encouraging consequence of this is that the teacher, far from being superseded by the computer, emerges as a key contributor to the situation. Even when children are working independently the *teacher's way of framing and organising the situation* affects how they operate [my emphasis].

Many factors will influence children's learning at the computer, but children's talk will be educationally effective if the children have been taught how to discuss things together, and if they are aware that appropriate talk is one of their aims. Children can be helped to understand that the way they talk to one another is one of the most important parts of their work together. They can be taught that spoken language is a tool for interthinking, and that such talk benefits both their group work and their own development.

Social influences, such as gender and friendship ties, may affect talk around the computer and in encouraging exploratory talk the teacher can help the children to work in groups less affected by such forces. Children's strong motivation to work at the computer means that computer activities offer an unrivalled opportunity to practise critical reasoning, a way of thinking that will serve them well in all curriculum areas and life beyond school.

Further reading

Dawes, L., Mercer, N. and Wegerif, R. (2000) *Thinking Together: A programme of activities for developing thinking skills at KS2*. Birmingham: Questions Publishing.

Mercer, N. (2000) *Words and Minds*. London: Routledge.

Swann, J. (1992) *Girls, Boys and Language*. London: Blackwell.

CHAPTER 6

Monitoring and Assessing Speaking and Listening in the Classroom

Introduction

As teachers you have responsibility for monitoring children's progress and keeping records of their development. Talking to our students about assessment we found that many felt less confident about doing this in speaking and listening than they did in other areas. They were aware of the need to incorporate assessment into their planning but often felt that they had few models to follow and that they were not sure what constituted evidence or how to capture and record it appropriately. As we have shown throughout this book, speaking and listening are all-pervasive: they are the means by which children learn and at the same time develop their spoken language competence. You may find disentangling the different strands challenging as you try to identify what counts as evidence of development and progression, both for individuals and for your class as a whole. Different aspects of talk can be identified: the social, the communicative, the cultural and the cognitive, all of which are affected by audience, purpose, context and content (Bearne and Elding 1996: 13). Other factors such as gender, personality, interests and confidence in whatever language is used will influence the way speakers behave. You will need to take these interrelated aspects of speaking and listening into consideration as you develop teaching strategies which incorporate different approaches to assessment.

Planning for assessment of Speaking and Listening

National Curriculum Programmes of Study and level descriptions for Speaking and Listening are rather generalised. We have to develop a range of strategies for listening to children talking, taking into account a number of features which might not relate to their oral ability. These will include:

- who the child is speaking to
- what sort of task is involved
- previous experience of the talk task
- the child's fluency in a home language as well as English
- the gender of the child and other group members.

We have to note the child's proficiency as a speaker and listener in a very wide range of situations. During a school day they will be required to respond to questions, listen to stories, act on oral instructions, work closely with their classmates and perhaps contribute to class discussion. We need to keep some record of their spoken interactions during the normal classroom day across different curriculum areas. This will involve collecting information on each child from a range of contexts and groupings, over time and will require a level of observation and recording which can at times seem daunting.

It may be helpful to have a checklist for recording Speaking and Listening activities and to consider some of the following factors:

- what the child knows and understands about the way language works
- the ability to communicate one to one, in or to a small or large group
- the ability to communicate with known and unknown audiences
- the appropriateness of language used in different circumstances
- the ability to interest an audience
- the ability to cooperate, take turns and not to dominate
- confidence, clarity, coherence, audibility
- range, variety and appropriateness of vocabulary
- the ability to reason, argue and debate
- the ability to summarise
- the ability to listen to others in different situations
- the ability to use speech in role play
- the ability to ask questions.

(from Browne 1996: 224)

Accounting for all of these requires meticulous recording. The pressure of National Curriculum testing on classroom teachers is considerable; as there is no formal oral test at either Key Stage 1 or Key Stage 2, priority may not be given to the assessment of Speaking and Listening. Reading and Writing may seem to have more status. And because, in the past, schools have not been required to provide evidence of progression to the same extent as they have for Reading and Writing, teachers may feel less confident about assigning levels and identifying aspects of progression. The SCAA publication and video, *Speaking and Listening: Key Stages 1 to 3, Levels 1 to 8. Exemplification of Standards* (SCAA 1996b) addresses this issue. Video extracts show examples of children in different contexts and identify aspects of their speaking and listening which are significant at particular levels. It illustrates the broad lines of progression that are expected: confidence in adapting talk, using standard English when appropriate, listening with understanding, participation in discussion. The video and accompanying document give a general idea of what is required by the Programmes of Study for Speaking and Listening in the National Order for English.

In response to the National Curriculum Orders, we need a focused approach which sees that planning for effective and informative assessment of Speaking and Listening is central to teaching and learning. We must also be aware that:

Making progress in talk isn't just a matter of practising different kinds of purposes for talk, or having experience of a number of audiences, or even having experience of all the types of talk text listed in curriculum documents. Making progress involves more socially and culturally influenced qualities, like growing flexibility and developing the ability to choose how and whether to speak in specific circumstances, the confidence to initiate discussion or support opinion by reference to wider experience. All of these elements linked to talk behaviours add to the range of what should be included in a challenging talk curriculum.

(Bearne and Elding 1996: 14)

The main purpose of teacher assessment is formative, its aim being to improve the quality of teaching and learning as it is taking place; summative judgments which are based on ongoing formative observation and recording will be passed on as feedback to pupils, parents and colleagues at the end of a term or Key Stage. All the information you record will also provide diagnostic evidence that highlights individual strengths or difficulties and will be the basis for your planning. Assessment should record what children can do and ideally be seen as a contract between you and the child. As far as possible, we should provide assessment procedures that allow children to be active participants in the process and to be able to reflect on their own speaking and listening. Some of the formats that we provide in this chapter are intended for this purpose.

It is clear that, for most children, there is an enormous expansion of learning capacity and language competence from pre-school years to the end of primary education. It is possible to chart some of the kinds of progression, from early to middle years at school, that are particularly evidenced in speaking and listening.

Baseline assessment: providing evidence of children's learning

It is evident that any assessment of pre-school children will have to take place through the medium of speaking and listening. As we have shown earlier in this book, children enter school with considerable experience of speaking and listening. The specification of goals for children's learning in the *Curriculum guidance for the foundation stage* (DfEE/QCA 2000) means that teachers of nursery children will have to plan and assess a range of activities to enable them to produce evidence of individual children's progress towards achieving the Early Learning Goals that will set them on track for Key Stage 1 of the National Curriculum. Much of this evidence will be obtained through dialogue between staff and children, and between children themselves.

A child's response during a single activity is not always an accurate or reliable guide to underlying competence. Therefore, there needs to be caution about conclusions drawn on the basis of one activity alone. Evidence collected over time from a range of activities is sometimes necessary in establishing what a child knows, understands and can do. Similarly, it is not always possible to infer what a child can do from observation alone, or recorded work alone. Talking with children has a central role in assessing their understanding, and it is often through talk that a fuller picture of what a child can do is gained.   (SCAA 1997a: 7)

The document *Curriculum guidance for the foundation stage* (DfEE/QCA 2000) is a guide for teachers in nursery units and in the early years of Key Stage 1. It covers areas such as planning, assessment and teaching and sets out what children and practitioners need to do in order to achieve the Early Learning Goals. The nature of the work in the early years means that there is an emphasis on speaking and listening particularly to provide evidence of learning and progression. The 'what' and the 'when' of assessment are not such an issue for teachers but the problem of 'how' remains, given the lack of time and the pressures of daily life in the classroom.

Assessment procedures in two nursery classes

Two nursery schools that we have observed are addressing this issue and recording children's development according to the six areas of learning set out in DfEE/QCA (2000):

- personal and social development;
- language and literacy;
- mathematics;
- knowledge and understanding of the world;
- physical development;
- creative development.

On their arrival in the school, a blank book is provided for each child in which their progress will be recorded. The first page consists of a photograph of the child at home and parents are invited to write down information about their child in response to such questions as, 'What does your child like to do at home?' 'Does your child play with other children?' 'Can you describe your child's personality?' Parents are also asked to write down what they expect their child to gain from the nursery. The book will gradually accumulate a series of photographs taken by the teacher or nursery nurse of the child at work, with written comments by the teacher on what the child is doing. Examples of the child's work, such as drawings, may also be included. A continuous record of the child's progress is being built up, which contributes to summative reports at the end of a year.

The purpose of these books is to record the child's development for the teacher, the parent and the child. The books are of a very personal nature and always available for the child and parent to refer to. Both schools find this an excellent way in which to involve parents in the nursery experience and become aware of their child's progress. There are many significant events during the day that parents do not see, such as playing with blocks, planting in the garden and mixing paints. All these can be photographed and serve as a reminder to teachers and help parents to see and understand what their child is learning in the nursery. One head teacher commented that the value of these books in the nursery was the way in which they could record a range of developments that happen so quickly at this age. Staff and parents can write in the record books; when one child won a swimming award his parent came into school and entered the award in his book. As children are working, staff can observe them, take photographs and note down on a label what the child is doing. Later, the teacher will write by the photograph in the book what the child has been learning in terms of the Desirable Learning Outcomes; targets are set for the child and the evidence of progression is noted. Records are entered in the children's books in the following way:

- observations are made and written in black
- analysis of learning and targets are written in red
- progression is written in green.

Evidence of progression might be that a child becomes able to write their name or when a child speaks in English instead of the community language for the first time. One head teacher, in a nursery school where a number of the children speak English and Panjabi, described how a boy had come to tell her about another child, 'He's speaking in Panjabi, that's Panjabi'. The head teacher recorded this evidence of the child's developing awareness of language. The arrival of a new set of photographs of the children at work provides a talking point, deciding which ones to put in their books and what was happening at the time. Children are able to write in the books and can contribute a drawing; in this way they share in the assessment process.

Both head teachers stressed the importance of this kind of detailed observation in order to record the process of learning rather than focusing on the end product. Although recording this kind of evidence is time consuming – the books are written by staff each week – the benefits are considered valuable by both schools. Parents are particularly enthusiastic about the record books and become highly motivated to contribute to them.

The record books are confidential to staff, parents and children and are freely available for parent or child to read and contribute to. Children love to look at them and often 'read' them during the day. The record books belong to the parent and child and at the end of their time in the nursery the books are taken home and can be shown to the next school.

Frameworks for assessment

Assessment procedures which involve children and their parents or carers in the process can be continued in Key Stage 1 classrooms. One of the most innovative and influential frameworks for the recording and assessment of language development, the Inner London Education Authority's Primary Language Record (Barrs *et al.* 1988), provided a framework for assessment which included input from parents and children. This would seem to be particularly useful in the case of speaking and listening where so much of the child's experience takes place in the home. This record encouraged a two-way communication between home and school, 'to let parent(s) share their knowledge of the child at home and school' (Barrs *et al.* 1988: 12) and required that the child should 'talk about and discuss with the teacher her/his experiences, achievements and interests as a language user' (Barrs *et al.* 1988: 14).

Despite the fact that this was written more than 12 years ago, many of the observations about the problems that are raised when we try to assess development in speaking and listening have not been resolved. 'Keeping a record of children's development in talking and listening may present difficulties not found when recording children's development as readers and writers' (Barrs *et al.* 1988: 20). One of the problems that the Primary Language Record identified was that 'talk disappears into the air'; another was that as teachers we are often part of any classroom interaction both as contributor and as monitor. Added to this is the fact that for many children in our classrooms who are using community languages as well as English, we may not be able to take into account the part played by their first language. More than a decade ago the writers of the record felt that 'adequate ways of mapping children's spoken language development have always proved elusive, mainly because of the complexity of what it is that is being analysed' (Barrs *et al.* 1988: 21). Alan Howe (1997: 61) wrote of the difficulties and constraints that beset the assessment of classroom talk:

- the pressure of numbers
- the ephemerality of the medium
- the power that context has over the behaviour, confidence and language use of the participants
- the way in which such behaviour can further alter the context.

In one sense, all we can hope for is a system of assessment that recognises the need to give all pupils a chance to reveal and to develop their spoken language competence, and which therefore gathers evidence over time and over as wide a range of authentic contexts as possible (Howe 1997: 61).

Gathering evidence of progress in speaking and listening, therefore, would seem to depend on creating our own frameworks. In the next part of this chapter we will discuss some of the ways in which we can use National Curriculum and SCAA guidelines to help us to keep a record of individual progress in our classrooms, which will also include the children as active participants in the process.

Recording evidence

The National Curriculum for English details the range of purposes for which talk opportunities should be provided in schools, and the key skills necessary for confident expression and careful listening. It also provides information about the development of pupils' use and appreciation of standard English and other dialects, and their growing fluency with an increasingly enriched vocabulary as they progress through the levels of attainment. In order to collect evidence of speaking and listening you will need to become confident about your own judgement of individual progress and you will almost certainly need to use some form of framework for recording progress. It is helpful to have some ideas of formats for recording in mind when you are planning the curriculum so that assessment for Speaking and Listening is incorporated into a term's work. Some record-keeping formats are included in this chapter. These are intended to help you to organise and structure your observations in order to identify strengths and areas for development. They have been adapted from a range of different sources and you will need to adapt them yourself to suit the particular needs of your own pupils.

We can create assessment opportunities by planning to listen to children talking in many different contexts, for different purposes and to different audiences over a period of time; in these contexts we also observe the child as a listener. You will need to consider the range of assessment opportunities available and different ways of recording evidence. There are many formal and informal situations in which information about an individual's speaking and listening abilities can be collected and recorded.

Teacher assessment

An initial assessment of children's speaking and listening skills might begin by considering readily observable features of talk. Table 6.1 is adapted from NOP (1991). This could be used on a single occasion or to gather information over a longer period.

The questions included in Table 6.1 could be asked in ways which would elicit a more detailed response. For example question 2, 'Does the child listen carefully?' could be expanded.

Table 6.1 What am I looking for in the child's talk?

		Yes	No
1	Does the child initiate and carry on conversations?		
2	Does the child listen carefully?		
3	Can the child's talk be easily understood?		
4	Does the child describe experiences?		
5	Does the child give instructions?		
6	Does the child follow verbal instructions?		
7	Does the child ask questions?		
8	Can the child contribute to a working group?		
9	Does the child 'think aloud'?		
10	Does the child modify talk for different audiences?		

Does the child listen carefully:

- to a familiar adult?
- to an unfamiliar adult?
- to friends?
- to unfamiliar children?
- when working in a group?
- in a whole-class situation?
- in a whole-school situation?

Each of the other questions could be expanded in a similar way in order to obtain more detailed information, depending on the purpose of the assessment at the time. You will need to think about the aims and purposes of recording and assessment of talk when deciding which method to use. You might like to consider these points:

- What is the aim of the assessment?
- What factual information is required?
- Who will look at or use the information that is collected?
- Will any action be taken as a result?
- In what form is the information required?
- How will this assessment help the child?

Different purposes will require different sorts of assessment. You might, for example, want to do a quick initial overview of your new class, or you might need a more detailed procedure that will enable you to monitor and chart their progress over a period of time, or you may need to carry out a detailed study of an individual child to support an application for a Statement of Special Need in Education.

Table 6.2 provides a straightforward way of monitoring classroom talk opportunities over a length of time. The time span chosen should be long enough to provide evidence from a balanced range of different contexts.

Self-assessment

Involving children in the assessment of their own speaking and listening helps them to develop a way of describing their own talk and become aware of the way they interact with other people. It also helps them to take an active part in their own learning as we saw in Chapter 5, where children became aware of themselves as talkers as they learned to work together round the computer.

The role of considering and recording their own talk can be provided by completing a 'talk diary'. This can build up a picture of children's talking and listening activities over a finite length of time in a way that is straightforward for both teacher and child to use and interpret. In the same way that reading records are constantly updated, adding to the content of a talk diary should be simple and frequent. A comprehensive talk diary can fulfil several purposes. It can:

Table 6.2 Monitoring classroom talk

Date	Context	Group names	Notes

- provide an overview of the range of opportunities for speaking and listening which the child has experienced
- record the child's strengths and weaknesses in speaking and listening
- build up a picture over time of speaking and listening activities
- focus the child's attention on the value of speaking and listening
- provide evidence for informal ongoing assessment
- contribute to planning of activities
- provide a resource for reporting the child's achievements.

Table 6.3 is a talk diary for upper primary pupils and is an example of a diary designed for children at Key Stage 2 to fill in themselves at the end of a week. The teacher can add any comments or notes that she feels might contribute more information or encourage a particular aspect of the child's talk. A diary such as this can be used for a week at intervals as a way of sampling children's perceptions of their talk behaviour or it can be used as continuous assessment. It illustrates for the child the range of skills and different contexts that are involved in speaking and listening.

Table 6.4 is a talk diary and is intended for use with younger children. It can be completed independently or with the teacher, but at first it would be useful to complete it with one child, or a small group of children, so that they can begin to consider and value a range of skills that they may not have realised they were using. This list is fairly comprehensive but you might want to adjust it so that you could discuss particular aspects with the whole class to raise their expectations of what we, as teachers, are looking for when we ask them to take part in Speaking and Listening activities. Talking to them fairly regularly about the way they feel about themselves as talkers will also provide further evidence of their developing skills in speaking and listening.

Describing progression

Learning about talk, how to talk, how to listen, and about the languages which we use to talk, is a complex procedure. Progress is made at different rates as different contexts and learning situations occur. The National Curriculum level descriptions identify aspects of speaking and listening which can act as markers to allocate the child to a level. We have adapted the level descriptions to provide a slightly simplified version which might help you to reach a decision about the level reached by a particular child.

Assigning an appropriate level

This assessment is to be undertaken in two stages. To begin with the child and teacher complete Table 6.5 together. This focuses children's attention on details of their attitudes and abilities as speakers and listeners. The interview also allows children to reflect on the criteria by which they are being judged and provides an opportunity for learning about speaking and listening. Some children will be capable of, and will benefit from,

Table 6.3 Talk Diary Key Stage 2: Page 1 of 2

Name: Start date: End date:

This week at school I have joined in by talking in these ways:

	Week 1	Week 2	Week 3	Week 4
discussing				
planning				
storytelling				
presenting work				
explaining				
reading aloud				
describing				
using new words				

This week I have tried to:

	Week 1	Week 2	Week 3	Week 4
listen carefully				
join in discussions				
speak confidently				
ask questions				
learn new words				
understand others				

I spoke and listened to:

	Week 1	Week 2	Week 3	Week 4
people in my class				
other children				
class teacher				
other teachers				
other school staff				
visitors				

Table 6.3 Talk Diary Key Stage 2: Page 2 of 2

A record of talking and listening: T = 'I talked'; L = 'I listened'

	Week 1	Week 2	Week 3	Week 4
whole–school assembly				
year or class assembly				
whole–class discussion				
group talk with adult				
group chosen by teacher				
friendship group				
other group				
working at the computer				
e-mail or telephone				
working in science				
working in maths				
working in English				
circle time or PSE				
tape or video recording				
drama				

Topics and contexts: What did I talk about? What did I listen to?

Week 1

Week 2

Week 3

Week 4

Table 6.4 Talk Diary Key Stage 1

This week in school:

	Week 1	Week 2	Week 3	Week 4
I talked to the class				
I listened in class				
I asked a question				
I answered a question				
I learned some new words				
I talked to my friends				
I talked in a work group				
I said 'please' and 'thank you'				

This is what I think about speaking and listening:

	Week 1	Week 2	Week 3	Week 4
I am good at talking				
I listen carefully				
People listen to what I say				
I can tell a story				
I can talk about things that happen to me				
I would rather listen than talk				
I can tell people how to do things				
I speak politely				
I find out things by listening				
I can say why I said something				
I know when to stop talking				
I can tell when words rhyme				
I am a quiet person				
I try to think before I say things				
I remember things I am told				

Table 6.5 Talking and Listening: Agreed Assessment Interview

Code: N = never   S = sometimes   U = usually   AA = almost always   A = always

What I can do with talking and listening

	date:	date:	date:	date:
I listen carefully				
I try to listen carefully				
I speak clearly				
I learn and use new words				
I ask questions				
I join in class talk				
I join in group talk				
I talk about problems				
I listen to instructions				
I remember what I've read				
I can explain what I mean				
I take turns in discussions				
I know when words rhyme				
I can describe things				
I know when not to talk				

What I think about talking and listening

I think about who is listening to me when I talk				
I can give reasons for what I say				
I can ask other people for their reasons				
I think about other people's reasons and ideas				
I like reading aloud				
I like telling stories				
I can tell jokes				
I like telling about me				
I enjoy being in a play				
I'd rather listen than talk				
I like to talk to friends				
I enjoy reading aloud				

interviewing each other and collaborating to complete the interview. Once the interview has been completed, the teacher has data which can be used to circle the 'best fit' statements on Table 6.6 and determine the child's level.

Identifying and monitoring progress

Because speaking and listening are everyday features of classroom life it may be difficult to detect the rather subtle differences that indicate progress. Children whose personalities allow them the confidence to speak more often or more clearly can be assessed more readily than those who are less sure of themselves, which presents something of a paradox, since it is the 'latter who may require input or direct help in order to make progress. Table 6.7 has been adapted from a more detailed scale of progression drawn up by teachers who wanted record-keeping systems that would supplement National Curriculum level descriptions (Bearne and Elding 1996: 15). This table lists observable features of talk in order to build up a picture of the child's competence in this area, and so monitor progress. The profile that is obtained by using this format can identify significant gaps in competence.

Links with the English Curriculum and the National Literacy Strategy

Opportunities for assessing Speaking and Listening occur in a range of different contexts within the English Curriculum, many of which have been illustrated in earlier chapters. Storytelling, reading aloud, sharing poems, drama activities, listening to tapes and watching videos, collaborative writing and research, reporting and explaining, all provide opportunities for assessment. These contexts allow the child to talk and listen for an increasing range of purposes but need to be included in the overall planning of provision which integrates Reading and Writing in such a way that clear links can be made with Speaking and Listening. SCAA (1997b: 6) stressed the importance of including Speaking and Listening as well as Reading and Writing in the teaching of literacy. The NLS framework (DfEE 1998c) has a more explicit focus on reading and writing, but it also raises the issue of the importance of speaking and listening.

Optional assessment of Speaking and Listening at Year 4

National assessment at Key Stage 2 has been problematic. In response to teachers' concerns, optional assessment units have been trialled and are available from QCA for schools to use at about half-way through Key Stage 2. These are intended to

Table 6.6 Summary of National Curriculum Speaking and Listening level descriptions

	Listening	Talk clarity	Vocabulary
Level 1	Listens to others Usually responds appropriately	Audible	Simple
Level 2	Listens carefully Responds appropriately	Clear	Increasing
Level 3	Listens confidently in more contexts	Confident	More varied
Level 4	Listens carefully in discussions	Confident in more contexts	Developing
Level 5	Can speak and listen in more formal contexts	Clear in a wide range of contexts	Varied vocabulary and expression
Level 6	Adapts to the demands of different situations	Fluent	Shows variety and fluency

	Discussion	Explanation	Further clarification
Level 1	Conveys meaning	Provides some detail	Beginning to extend ideas
Level 2	Shows awareness of others	Includes some relevant detail	Starts to adapt vocabulary and tone to context
Level 3	Shows understanding of main points	Begins to adapt talk to the needs of the listener	Some awareness of Standard English. Can explain and communicate ideas
Level 4	Asks questions and responds to the views of others	Talk is adapted to the purpose	Some use of Standard English. Develops ideas thoughtfully and conveys opinions clearly
Level 5	Pays close attention, asks questions, and takes account of others	Engages the interest of the listener by inclusion of detail	Beginning to use Standard English appropriately. Responsive to ideas
Level 6	Takes an active part, shows understanding and sensitivity	Increasingly interesting through variety of expression	Usually fluent in Standard English in formal situations. Increasingly confident

Table 6.7 Observable features of talk

		date	date	date
Beginning Speaker and Listener who can:				
Working towards Level 1	communicate			
	understand simple verbal instructions			
	answer questions			
	join in with a group			
Improving Speaker and Listener who can:				
Levels 1 to 2	tell a story from pictures			
	talk about the contents of books			
	convey a simple message			
	ask clearly for things			
	talk with friends			
	ask relevant questions			
Competent Speaker and Listener who can:				
Level 3	tell a story they have made up			
	join in class and group discussion			
	convey a verbal reply to a message			
	recall and recount personal experiences			
	notice words that rhyme			
	explain the work they are doing			
	discuss familiar issues			
Experienced Speaker and Listener who can:				
Levels 4 to 5	explain ideas and stories in sequence			
	make up questions			
	recall events for an audience			
	consider listeners when talking			
	listen to and reflect on the views of others			
	be prepared to take turns in talk			
	ask critical questions in discussions			
Fluent Speaker and Listener who can:				
Level 6	explain ideas and stories in sequence			
	understand simple verbal instructions			
	give opinions based on reasons			
	discuss a variety of topics			
	show verbal confidence in many contexts			
	initiate and sustain conversation			

complement and support existing assessment procedures being used by schools. The Assessment Units for English, Maths and Science have been designed to support schools in planning for the second half of Key Stage 2 but may also be used for curriculum development purposes. Unlike the Key Stage 2 Statutory Assessment which is, by definition, summative assessment and monitored externally, these Assessment Units offer teachers an opportunity to produce evidence of children's attainment that can be used to complement existing assessment procedures. It is proposed that evidence of children's achievement at this stage will be used to inform planning and target setting.

Unlike the Key Stage 2 Statutory Assessment, these assessment units include Speaking and Listening, taking into account the fact that the Programmes of Study for English emphasise the use of effective spoken language. The assessment units for Speaking and Listening at Year 4 focus on:

- using Standard English where appropriate
- adaptation of style for meaning and effect
- listening with understanding, responding to others' ideas
- participation in discussion, taking turns and making a range of relevant contributions (QCA 1997).

The units of work for Speaking and Listening provide opportunities for teachers to gather information on these aspects and use it to supplement their own assessment. Two units of work support the teaching, learning and assessment of Speaking and Listening. These are demanding, whole-class activities; the first requiring the teacher to set up a role play in which the children discuss a proposal to exclude traffic from a town centre; the second to work in small groups to prepare a short taped tour guide of their school. The children will be involved in the assessment process, using a series of Talk Logs which include both group and self-assessment questions. For example:

- How well did people in your group explain their ideas/give reasons/listen to each other? How well did you keep in your role?
- Shade in the bubbles to show what you think you did well at. (The 'bubbles' are speech balloons enclosing statements such as: listening to others/working in a pair/explaining ideas/leading a group/asking questions/taking turns/helping others/presenting ideas in a large group/helping the group do well (QCA/97/021).

The second activity involves preparing a tape-recording, completing a planning sheet and an evaluation of a guide prepared by another group, commenting on the following points: easy to follow directions/helpful for a new pupil/clear speaker/sounds welcoming/interesting details/lively presentation (QCA/97/022).

The aim of the first unit is to provide an activity that will develop children's ability to express an informed point of view, in both group and whole-class discussions. Assessment focuses on:

- collaborative skills, e.g. turn-taking, listening and responding to other people's views, asking and answering questions, supporting the work of the group;
- the ability to argue and support a point of view in discussion;
- the ability to present opinions clearly and in spoken standard English.

The second unit has a different focus and aims to develop the use of the spoken word to plan and present work and the assessment focuses on:

- the ability to give clear directions;
- clarity of delivery;
- awareness of the needs of the listener.

For the first unit, evidence is provided by the use of teachers' Observation Sheets and children's Talk Logs; for the second unit, evidence is provided by children's taped commentaries, teachers' Observation Sheets and the children's Evaluation Sheets. The units provide detailed criteria to help teachers to make the 'best fit' between the children's work and level descriptions.

Clearly this approach to the assessment of specific and very structured activities of this kind will provide a model for the assessment of Speaking and Listening in both Key Stages 1 and 2. The success of such activities in Year 4 will depend on pupils' previous experience of working in similar ways and teachers' confidence about planning and organising their classes for Speaking and Listening. The introduction to Year 4 Assessment Unit 2 makes this clear:

> For the activity to be successful, it is important that children are given plenty of opportunity to explore, develop, explain and defend their ideas. It works best if they have already had experience of working in mixed gender and ability groups, and in whole-class discussion. There is an element of drama to the activity taking on different roles, and teachers should give plenty of encouragement and support as children begin to explore their roles and develop ideas.   (QCA/97/021: 3)

This chapter has described ways in which assessment can be planned at the same time as learning activities. This should enable you to organise your classroom and resources in a way that makes the value of talk explicit to children. Careful organisation will create suitable conditions for observing, assessing and recording children's competence as speakers and listeners. A process of continuous assessment can be usefully integrated into the children's language experiences.

Conclusion

In early years classrooms, children's curriculum-related learning can be assessed through the medium of spoken language. At this stage, children are beginning to use spoken language as a tool for learning. As they talk about new ideas and new knowledge with others, they increase their vocabulary, extend their talk repertoire, and become increasingly aware of the different demands made by different tasks and contexts. The purpose of assessment is to monitor both the understanding of curriculum knowledge and the ability to express this appropriately. Assessment must recognise spoken language as the child's most valuable tool for learning.

Further reading

Bearne, E. and Elding, S. (1996) 'Speaking and listening. Describing progress', *Primary English Magazine* 2(2), 15–19.

Clarke, S. (2000) *Targeting Assessment in Primary Classrooms*. London: Hodder & Stoughton.

Clarke, S. (2001) *Unlocking Formative Assessment*. London: Hodder & Stoughton.

Howe, A. (1997) *Making Talk Work*. Sheffield: National Association for the Teaching of English (NATE).

Epilogue

Listening to children

Three six-year-old girls look at photographs:

23. Let me have a look at this one
24. It's dark
25. The wind . . .
26. Very dark
27. The sea's . . .
28. The sea's all wavy
29. Yeah
30. Wavy and . . .
31. Dull, dull
32. Yeah, it's really dull
33. Dark, very muddy . . .
34. Cold, dark, wet.
    . . . .
85. I know, the waves are coming up onto the ground, the land, aren't they?
86. Wavy
87. The waves are coming up onto the ground
88. Yeah
89. It's muddy, very muddy
90. Yeah, muddy
91. That's the sea
92. Yeah
93. Floody, tuddy, puddy
94. Puddles
95. Yeah, lots of puddles

These young children are playing with language and sound, producing a polyphonic counterpoint of repetition that is close to poetry.

96. The moon isn't there
97. It's dark and cold
98. Look at that light
99. That light's fallen off
100. Dropping, dropping
101. 'Cos the wet drops off the trees
102. The rocks are falling into the sea
103. Where?
104. Look that one's sinking
105. The wind's blowing very hard
106. Yeah
107. Twisting, twisting . . .
108. The waves are twisting around
109. Yeah
110. The leaves are twisting 'cos the wind, they go round and round

A group of trainees in the fourth year of a Primary BEd degree course were required to set a task which would involve children in collaborative talk. They could do this in any curriculum area but were to transcribe an extract that provided evidence of the children working together. Rosemary's class was engaged in a geography topic on weather; she wanted to give them an activity that would encourage group discussion and collaboration while developing geographical knowledge and understanding. The children were aged six in a Reception/Year 1/Year 2 class of 25 in a rural lower school. The three girls above were recorded as they looked at photographs of windy weather. They were talking so excitedly that Rosemary was not always able to identify the speakers but she was able to identify the way that their talk was developing. At first, they used a listing type of discussion, a pattern of statement and response (Phillips 1988) which in this case was descriptive. This demonstrated their knowledge of the conventions of turn-taking. As they continued, they became more hesitant and thoughtful. Looking at lines 27 to 34, Rosemary felt that their repetition of words permitted continuity and development of the discussion. As they progressed, she noticed a marked change in the style of the talk. One child digressed from the main focus of the photographs and initiated a period of sustained collaborative talk. Rosemary commented on the extract, to show how this happened:

51. A: Butterflies are not around, flowers are growing, flowers are growing
    (*Said with certainty – this initiates the topic*)

52. B: No they're not
    (*The first sign of disagreement*)

53. B: Flowers are dying, getting old and . . .
    (*Now hesitant and uncertain*)

54. B: No, they're not . . .
    (*Attempts to raise her status as the authority and take control*)

55. C: They're not dying. How can flowers die?
   (*C accepts B's position. Her question moves the talk on*)

56. B: Yes they can

57. A: Yeah, not like people die, they don't die the same as people
   (*This digression leads to further development*)

58. C: It's really dark
   (*This attempt to bring group back 'on task' fails*)

59. A: People could die, because they are really cold and then they die . . .
   (*A perseveres with her argument which leads to reasoning*)

60. C: It's raining
   (*C tries again with more success*)

61. B: It looks like that pole's fallen over, doesn't it?
   (*Her question invites further comment on the task and indicates the end of the sub-topic. She assumes control of the discussion*)

62. Yeah

63. Yeah (*She accepts B's control and gets back 'on task'*)

Rosemary's analysis of this extract shows the development of relationships in the group.

A proposes new ideas questioningly and looks for reassurance or confirmation. B takes on the mantle of authority: C has little involvement but attempts to keep the group on task. In this section of the discussion, A demonstrates further progress in her attempts to used reasoned argument as she adopts a position that is more questioning and investigatory.

Rosemary looks at the transcript as a whole and identifies steady progress from the early stage of listing descriptive observations to this more collaborative, exploratory talk.

Initially their talk focuses solely on the visual effects of the wind:
Look, trees have fallen down/And that sign's fallen off/Buildings are falling down/Trees are waving round. This soon develops, becoming more descriptive and using language appropriate for describing the weather:

15. It's wet, miserable
16. Foggy
32. Yeah, it's really dull
34. Cold, dark, wet

Their talk demonstrates their knowledge of the need for appropriate clothing to suit the climatic conditions. We can see from the following comments that they are applying their own experiences to the situation captured in the photograph:

70. He's got his coat on
71. And he's got his warm cagoule

81. He's got his warm joggers on and his boots
82. Yeah, he's got his boots on, his wet boots

128. He hasn't got any gloves on
129. Well his hands can't be cold, can they?

Using this carefully documented evidence, Rosemary was able to make some tentative observations about what this group was learning. She was able to assess the children in two ways; first looking at their use of spoken language and then at the knowledge and understanding that was evident through their talk.

It was evident from an assessment of their talk, as recorded in the transcript, that the group was functioning in the following ways. They:

• had confidence in their talking and listening;
• listened to each other;
• were listened to and understood by the others;
• used language appropriately in order to convey meaning;
• related their own experiences to a new context;
• spoke with clarity.

These factors would suggest that as a group the children are 'gaining experience as speaker/listener' (Bearne and Elding 1996) and that using National Curriculum level descriptors, they would be around Level 1 to 2. Child A demonstrates further skills in her talk – she initiates ideas and is able to formulate a reasoned argument – in doing so she reveals abilities that are almost certainly Level 2.

Assessment through talk shows geographical knowledge and understanding in a number of areas: the visual effects of the wind; directionality; climatic conditions and how these affect physical and human features; and the necessity for appropriate clothing.

Their ability to use appropriate vocabulary to describe physical and human features and to select and use information from the photographs and express their views on the environments shown, indicates that they are, as a group at Level 2 in their geographical skills and understanding. The evidence would suggest that Child C is probably at Level 1 and progressing to Level 2 (DfE 1995b).

Interestingly, much geographical thinking was taking place throughout the group discussion that was not revealed in their talk. It was only upon reflection when they were reporting their findings back to the class that these became apparent. It would seem that this is not an unusual occurrence, 'their talk often provides surprisingly little information about what learning is taking place – it is "in their heads". But when you ask them to report back, you will get many valuable insights' (NOP 1991: 17). Indeed, when this group reported back, they demonstrated a greater level of geographical language, using a range of terminology to describe the wind. They also remarked on evidence of the strength of the wind and gave reasons for their statements. In addition they also made reasoned attempts to place the photograph within a global perspective.

Rosemary concluded that this assessment had suggested ways in which she might provide future opportunities for group work of this kind: 'This will mean working in pairs or small groups, initially, to develop thoughts, ideas and language and then sharing their findings, possibly in a whole-class setting or through the use of other group strategies, such as "jigsawing".' She felt that talk needed to be planned for, supported and encouraged across the curriculum as part of a whole-school approach, since:

> In adult life and in the world of work talk is far more important than reading or writing... If schools neglect talk they will not only deny young people a vital means of learning but they will be failing to equip them for life.   (Jones 1988: 29)

Returning to Rosemary's transcript, it is interesting to observe how this group, with little previous experience of working in this way, was able to draw to a satisfactory conclusion:

113. The animals are hibernating
114. Yeah
115. I thought that was . . .
116. The letter box has fallen down
117. That's not a letter box
118. There's no summer birds
119. Yeah, there's no birds
120. Because there isn't, because they're all nesting
121. With their pillows
122. They haven't got pillows
123. With their hay
124. No, with their grass
125. They're laying in their . . . and, and finding new nests
126. Yeah
127. And it's not sunny
128. He hasn't got any gloves on
129. Well his hands can't be cold, can they?
130. He's got his coat zipped up
131. Rabbits are going in their holes, cats are going inside
132. Yeah
133. Ducks, what are they doing?
134. Um . . .
135. They're going into the farmyard and hibernating and . . .

136. Ducks don't hibernate!
137. And elephants, they are lying down and . . .
138. Goats, they are hibernating. All the animals
139. Hedgehogs are rolling up in balls
140. The foxes are hibernating (*Giggles*)
141. I think we have said enough now
142. No, no one is going outside. They're all staying in their houses 'cos it's so windy

Lynda, who was also working with very young children, was concerned that National Curriculum requirements suggest a shift in emphasis from informal talk to more formal speaking, a performance mode that does not share some of the features that characterise the kind of talk that occurs in collaborative learning situations, 'short turns, unfinished sentences, interruptions and occasional uses of anecdote to make a point'. Teachers need to be aware of these differences when they are assessing children's talk. In her analysis of a transcript of three five-year-olds' collaborative talk, Lynda was looking for evidence of learning, of how they were using language to communicate, receive meaning and make sense of the task she had set. She wanted the group, two girls and a boy, to develop a narrative together – a more ambitious project than those described by the students in Chapter 3. Taking their age and lack of experience into consideration, she hoped to do this through role play.

> I chose role play because it can make a valuable contribution towards developing children's confidence in speaking and listening and narrative because it is a powerful device for making sense of experience as children will bring what they know and what they are learning about life and living to these situations. (Graham and Kelly 2000: 79)

She started them off by asking them to close their eyes and imagine a beautiful shop full of toys including a rag doll with big eyes.

A: I can see it (*excitedly*) I can see her with a hat
G: I can see her with beautiful eyes . . . like my shoes
S: I can see short hair on her
A: She's got lipstick on her mouth. She's got bracelets on her hands and she's got blusher on her face and she's got fing . . . finger things
G: She's got nail varnish
A: Yes (*nodding approvingly*) nail varnish

In her analysis of the talk that followed, Lynda observed that they moved on from this rather polite turn-taking, simply describing things, to collaborative decision making. At first, as ideas were formed in quick succession, the children wanted to express them immediately and turn-taking was controlled by interrupting others, 'I want to talk', but as the role play developed they seemed to be swept along by the story they were jointly creating with help from Lynda who took part in role as a broken toy:

Teacher: The toy mender is not mending us...what are we going to do about it?

G: Nobody will be able to buy us and no one will think you are pretty and they would say 'that doll is not very nice, so I am not going to buy that one. I'm going to buy the pretty one'. That is me

S: Why don't we get the...hammers and tools...go get tools...hammers and fix us?

G: Oh yes

A: Why don't we walk out and get some more tools and spoons and take all our stuffing out with a spoon?

G: If you don't have anything to mend, then you should go to the next shop and buy some tools

S: He's left some tools here, a hammer and screws and screwdrivers

A: Mend legs with screws, put a nail in legs and scoop out the stuff, make another toy like us and we just put a button in it so it says our voices and then we can run out and buy some things

G: And then we could buy a book and look through the book until we find a mending piece then we just walk in the door and look out with our big eyes and say (*she stands up with arms outstretched*) 'Magical glue, magical magical glue, magical, magical, come to us magical we need some hammers and stuff for mending the head toy'

S: I've got a broken arm

G: So have I

S: Why don't we go to hospital...?

G: We could get some new shoes for me

A: Why don't we go to the shop and buy...get some...some things, new shoes and tools?

In a close analysis of the transcript of the whole episode, Lynda notes the children's different strengths. Referring to this extract, she suggests that:

S, although a more reluctant speaker initiates a lot of well thought-out ideas: 'hammers and tools' and includes the others in the suggestion, 'Why don't we...?' This suggestion receives instant approval from G, who recognises its validity and exclaims 'Oh yes!'. S's idea is taken up and expanded by A who repeats S's initial response, 'Why don't we...walk out and get some more tools and spoons...?' This shows how she listens and assimilates information and uses this as the basis to tentatively move the discussion on, suggesting how to use the tools.

Lynda demonstrates how they build on previous knowledge and experience to make sense of the task:

Most of the ideas come from their everyday life experience, 'I've got a broken arm', 'Why don't we go to hospital?'. However, when G elaborately describes an imaginative option as opposed to a practical solution to the dilemma...this suggestion is unchallenged and ignored, possibly it is not understood. G's talk characteristically shows little concern for the audience. A reshapes her ideas when they are not taken up by the others, 'tools and spoons' and reformulates them in a way that extends what others have suggested and makes them more acceptable, 'Mend legs with screws, put a nail in legs and scoop out the stuff', supports S's 'a hammer and screws and screwdrivers'. She adds nails to the group's collection of appropriate tools. In the final line of this extract she uses diplomacy; she is a cohesive force within the group and reveals a sophisticated level of thinking and reasoning.

Lynda's careful analysis of the children's talk allowed her to make an assessment of each child's progress:

A pattern of the way these children use talk and learn through talk emerges. S speaks very little, but what he does say is critical to the development of the task. His talk is littered with false starts and repetitions, which may suggest that he is holding his place whilst he is thinking (Maclure *et al.* 1988: 81). His thinking is practical and specific and shows evidence of an emerging problem-solving ability, but he neither supports nor challenges the others' viewpoints nor makes any reference to their proposals. A has a cohesive role in the group. She is able to evaluate S's contribution and support his ideas while forming her own. She listens intently and matches what she hears to what has been said previously and this informs what she says next. She obviously learns through listening and reflection although she only tentatively expresses her own ideas and may retract statements quickly if they are not immediately approved by the others, suggesting that she has a problem sustaining a point of view in discussion. G shows some imaginative creative thinking although this does not always follow a logical progression or the previous speaker's line of argument, as she does not always listen to the others. She seems to take the leading role because she has the strongest desire to make the discussion her own.

All the children show evidence of thinking which includes examples of hypothesising, predicting, exploring and evaluating ideas. Their understanding of the problem is evident through their talk which reflects and draws upon previous experience. Understanding seems to come about by matching abstract ideas with real scenarios; repetition helps them to shape ideas. Through their talk, which has explored imagined possibilities, the children will have become more adept at communication and collaborative decision-making, relevant not only to the drama session or to English but to all subjects.

At present, Speaking and Listening at Key Stages 1 and 2 is addressed entirely through teacher assessment. Rosemary and Lynda's systematic assessment of the children they were teaching shows how listening to children talking can 'give a more complete picture of children's attainment as language users' (NOP 1991: 61). Their meticulous analyses of what, at first, appeared to be rather random and daunting examples of small group interaction between very young children show the value of listening very carefully to what they are saying. They had learned a lot about the children's capabilities. However, we are not suggesting that assessment of talk should or could involve this kind of detailed analysis. It is a very time-consuming activity indeed. But being a fly on the wall and jotting down things that you overhear, observing and listening, allowing children to record and listen critically to themselves so that they begin to recognise their own strengths and the strategies that they are using, is possible and helpful as we have suggested in Chapters 5 and 6. Nor do we want to give the impression that small group talk is easy for the participants. Chapter 5 discusses some of the problems and suggests solutions.

Many of you will meet situations in school similar to those described by the students who were setting out to tackle this assignment. They had been asked 'What kind of evidence of learning can be drawn from an analysis of a transcript of children's collaborative talk?'. They often found that children were not used to working collaboratively; they needed structured help. Vyv was prepared to intervene when she felt that a Year 6 group who were working on their own could go further. They were using a set of questions (Chambers 1992) to talk about a novel; one question asked them to consider whether there were any 'hidden messages' in the text:

E: Morals, does it mean?
C: You think it's only a story, but as we said earlier, it could be true . . .
E: Well, I don't suppose it would be an 18 video rating because there's no bad language. But maybe, young children might think it'd be a good idea to run away
C: . . . and think oh good, let's run away . . .
E: . . . and play with matches
     (*Vyv, who has not been part of the discussion up to this point senses that they need help with the question*)
Vyv: OK, but what kind of messages, if any, do you think Ruth Thomas would like you to come away from the story with?

In her assignment, Vyv comments, 'For the first time, the discussion is marked by a silence of uncertainty and thought. All three group members look searchingly at each other'.

C: (*suddenly*) Oh, maybe they're saying, 'Don't do it'
S: Well, it could be that

And the discussion continues. Vyv, reflecting on the talk that she has transcribed and analysed, writes in her conclusion:

In the final analysis, it seems that talk as a medium through which to learn, is unique in the contribution it makes. Once basic talking skills and conventions are acquired, a wealth of collaborative learning can take place. Through exploratory talk, by sharing the entire group's skills, knowledge and understanding, the resulting learning which takes place, is somehow more than the sum of the group's knowledge. Learning is taken into another dimension, in which all members benefit from an enriched learning experience. By combining thoughts, ideas and insight, the end product, far from being simply the sum of its parts, emerges as a unique, enriching experience for each participant.

So we have ended this book as we began, with the thoughts of student teachers faced with the problems and pleasures of creating a classroom environment for speaking and listening. Each chapter has addressed different ways of responding creatively to all your pupils' needs in what is potentially the most immediate and satisfying aspect of working with children and the medium through which all your teaching will take place.

References

Anderson, H. and Hilton, M. (1997) 'Speaking subjects: the development of a conceptual framework for the teaching and learning of spoken language', *English in Education* 31(1), 12–23.

Baddeley, G. (1991) *Teaching Talking and Listening in Key Stage 2*. York: National Oracy Project (NOP)/National Curriculum Council (NCC).

Barnes, D. (1973) *Language in the Classroom. Educational Studies: A Second Level Course Language and Learning. Block 4*. Milton Keynes: Open University Press.

Barnes, D. (1976) *From Communication to Curriculum*. Harmondsworth: Penguin.

Barnes, D. and Sheeran, S. (1992) 'Oracy and genre: speech styles in the classroom', in Norman, K. (ed.) *Thinking Voices. The Work of the National Oracy Project*. London: Hodder & Stoughton.

Barnes, D., Britton, J. and Rosen, H. (1969) *Language, the Learner and the School*. Harmondsworth: Penguin.

Barrs, M. *et al.* (1988) *The Primary Language Record. Handbook for Teachers*. London: Centre for Language in Primary Education (CLPE).

Baumfield, V. (1996) 'Spiritual development. The power of the story', *Primary English Magazine* 1(2), 29–31.

Beard, R. (ed.) (1995) *Rhyme, Reading and Writing*. London: Hodder & Stoughton.

Bearne, E. and Elding, S. (1996) 'Speaking and listening. Describing progress', *Primary English Magazine* 2(2), 15–19.

Bennett, N. and Dunne, E. (1992) *Managing Classroom Groups*. London: Simon & Schuster.

Brice-Heath, S. (1983) *Ways with Words. Language, Life and Work in Communities and Classrooms*. Cambridge: Cambridge University Press.

Browne, A. (1996) *Developing Language and Literacy 3–8*. London: Paul Chapman Publishing.

Bruce, T. (1987) *Early Childhood Education*. London: Hodder & Stoughton.

Bruner, J. (1983) *Child's Talk*. Oxford: Oxford University Press.

Bruner, J. (1986) *Actual Minds, Possible Worlds*. Cambridge, Mass.: Harvard University Press.

Bryant, P. E. and Bradley, L. (1985) *Children's Reading Difficulties*. Oxford: Blackwell.

Bunting, R. (2000) *Teaching Language in the Primary Years*, 2nd edn. London: David Fulton Publishers.

Chambers, A. (1992) *Tell Me*. Stroud: The Thimble Press.

Clarke, S. (2000) *Targeting Assessment in Primary Classrooms*. London: Hodder & Stoughton.

Clarke, S. (2001) *Unlocking Formative Assessment*. London: Hodder & Stoughton.

Clay, M. M. (1979) *The Early Detection of Reading Difficulties*, 3rd edn. New Zealand: Heinemann.

Colwell, E. (1991) *Storytelling*. Stroud: The Thimble Press.

Corden, R. (1999) 'Shameful neglect: speaking, listening and literacy', *FORUM* 41(3).

Corden, R. (2000) *Literacy and Learning Through Talk. Strategies for the primary classroom.* Buckingham: Open University Press.

David, T. (1990) *Under Five – Under Educated?* Milton Keynes: Open University Press.

Dawes, L., Mercer, N. and Fisher, E. (1992) 'The quality of talk at the computer', *Language and Learning* (October).

Dawes, L., Mercer, N. and Wegerif, R. (2000) *Thinking Together: A programme of activities for developing thinking skills at KS2*. Birmingham: Questions Publishing.

Department for Education (DfE) (1995a) *The National Curriculum*. London: HMSO.

Department for Education (DfE) (1995b) *Geography in the National Curriculum*. London: HMSO.

Department for Education and Employment (DfEE) (1998a) *Requirements for Courses of Initial Teacher Training. Circular 4/98.* London: DfEE.

Department for Education and Employment (DfEE) (1998b) *Circular 4/98. Teaching: High Status, High Standards. Requirements for Courses of Initial Teacher Training*. London: DfEE.

Department for Education and Employment (DfEE) (1998c) *The National Literacy Strategy. Framework for Teaching*. London: DfEE.

Department for Education and Employment (DfEE)/Qualifications and Curriculum Authority (QCA) (1999) *The National Curriculum: Handbook for Primary Teachers in England and Wales*. London: DfEE/QCA.

Department for Education and Employment (DfEE)/Qualifications and Curriculum Authority (QCA) (2000) *Curriculum Guidance for the Foundation Stage*. London: DfEE/QCA.

Department of Education and Science (DES) (1975) *A Language for Life* (The Bullock Report). London: HMSO.

Department of Education and Science (DES) (1998) *Report of the Committee of Inquiry into the Teaching of English Language* (The Kingman Report). London: HMSO.

Des-Fountain, J. and Howe, A. (1992) 'Pupils Working together on understanding', in Norman, K. (ed.) *Thinking Voices. The Work of the National Oracy Project*. London: Hodder & Stoughton.

Dombey, H. (1992) 'Early lessons in reading narrative'. IEDPE Conference Barcelona, Imprime par l'Université Paris-Nord.

Donaldson, M. (1978) *Children's Minds*. London: Fontana.

Edwards, D. and Mercer, N. (1987) *Common Knowledge: The Development of Understanding in the Classroom*. London: Methuen/Routledge.

Elliot, J. (1991) *Action Research for Educational Change*. Milton Keynes: Open University Press.

Fisher, E. (1993) 'Distinctive features of pupil–pupil classroom talk and their relationship to learning: how discursive exploration might be encouraged', *Language and Education* 7(4) 239–57.

Fox, C. (1988) 'Poppies will make them grant', in Meek, M. and Mills, C. (eds) *Language and Literacy in the Primary School*, 53–68. Lewes: The Falmer Press.

Fox, C. (1989) 'Children thinking through story', *English in Education* 23(2), 25–36.

Fox, C. (1993) *At the Very Edge of the Forest. The Influence of Literature on Storytelling by Children*. London: Cassell.

Garton, A. and Pratt, C. (1989) *Learning to be Literate*. London: Blackwell.

Goodwin, P. (2001) (ed.) *The Articulate Classroom. Talking and Learning in the Primary School*. London: David Fulton Publishers.

Goswami, U. (1994) 'Phonological skills, analogies, and reading development', *Reading* 28(2), 32–7.

Goswami, U. and Bryant, P. E. (1990) *Phonological Skills and Learning to Read*. London: Lawrence Erlbaum Associates.

Graham, J. and Kelly, A. (2000) *Reading Under Control. Teaching Reading in the Primary School*, 2nd edn. London: David Fulton Publishers.

Grainger, T. (1997) *Traditional Storytelling in the Primary Classroom*. Leamington Spa: Scholastic.

Gregory, E. (1996) *Making Sense of a New World. Learning to Read in a Second Language*. London: Paul Chapman Publishing.

Grugeon, E. (1988) 'Children's oral culture: a transitional experience', in Maclure, M. *et al. Oracy Matters: The Development of Talking and Learning in Education*. Milton Keynes: Open University Press.

Grugeon, E. (1989) 'Becoming storytellers', *Early Years: Journal of TACTYC* 10(1), 10–15.

Grugeon, E. and Gardner, P. (2000) *The Art of Storytelling for Teachers and Pupils. Using Stories to Develop Literacy in Primary Classrooms*. London: David Fulton Publishers.

Grugeon, E., Rix, C. and Yiannaki, E. (1998) 'Finding the right words: some observations on learning to use the language of science', *Education 3–13* 26(1).

Gura, P. (ed.) directed by Bruce, T. (1992) *Exploring Learning: Young Children and Blockplay*. London: Paul Chapman Publishing.

Hammersley, M. (1993) 'On the teacher as researcher', in Hammersley, M. (ed.) *Educational Research: Current Issues*. London: Paul Chapman with the Open University.

Hollindale, P. (1997) *Signs of Childness in Children's Books*. Stroud: The Thimble Press.

Housego, E. and Burns, C. (1994) 'Are you sitting too comfortably? a critical look at "Circle Time" in primary classrooms', *English in Education* 28(2), 23–9.

Howe, A. (1997) *Making Talk Work*. Sheffield: National Association for the Teaching of English (NATE).

Howe, A. and Johnson, J. (1992) *Common Bonds: Storytelling in the Classroom*. London: Hodder & Stoughton.

Hughes, M. (1999) 'Oracy within the National Literacy Strategy', *English 4–11* 7.

James, F. (1996) *Phonological Awareness: Classroom Strategies*. Cheshire: United Kingdom Reading Association.

Jones, P. (1998) *Lipservice: The Story of Talk in Schools*. Milton Keynes: Open University Press.

Keiner, J. (1992) 'A brief history of the National Oracy Project', in Norman, K. (ed.) *Thinking Voices. The Work of the National Oracy Project*, 247–55. London: Hodder & Stoughton.

Literacy and Numeracy National Project (1997) *The National Literacy Project Draft Framework for Teaching*. London: HMSO.

Literacy Task Force (1997) *A Reading Revolution*. London: HMSO.

Maclure, M., Phillips, T. and Wilkinson, A. (eds) (1988) *Oracy Matters: The Development of Talking and Learning in Education*. Milton Keynes: Open University Press.

McTear, M. (1987) *Children's Conversation*. Oxford: Blackwell.

Meek, M. and Mills, C. (eds) (1988) *Language and Literacy in the Primary School*. Lewes: The Falmer Press.

Mercer, N. (1995) *The Guided Construction of Knowledge: Talk Amongst Teachers and Learners*. Clevedon: Multilingual Matters.

Mercer, N. (1996) 'The quality of talk in children's collaborative activity in the classroom', *Learning and Instruction* 6(4), 359–78.

Mercer, N. (2000) *Words and Minds. How we use language to think together*. London: Routledge.

Mills, R. and Mills, J. (1993) *Bilingualism in the Primary School: A Handbook for Teachers*. London: Routledge.

Mosley, J. (1993) *Turn Your School Round*. Cambridge: Learning Development Aids (LDA).

Mosley, J. (1996) *Quality Circle Time*. Cambridge: Learning Development Aids (LDA).

Mosley, J. (2000) *More Quality Circle Time*. Cambridge: Learning Development Aids (LDA).

Moyles, J. (ed.) (1994) *The Excellence of Play*. Milton Keynes: Open University Press.

National Association for the Teaching of English (NATE) (1996) 'News from NATE. Inspecting Talk', *Primary English Magazine* 2(1), 5.

National Literacy Strategy (NLS) (2000a) *Supporting Pupils Learning English as an Additional Language*. London: DfEE.

National Literacy Strategy (NLS) (2000b) *Grammar for Writing*. London: DfEE.

National Literacy Strategy (NLS) (2001) *Developing Early Writing*. London: DfEE.

National Oracy Project (NOP) (1991) 'Assessing Talk in Key Stages 1 and 2', *Occasional Papers in Oracy No. 5*. York: National Curriculum Council (NCC)/NOP.

Newsom, E. and Newsom, J. (1975) 'Intersubjectivity and the transmission of culture: on the social origins of symbolic functioning', *Bulletin of the British Psychological Society* 28.

Norman, K. (ed.) (1992) *Thinking Voices. The Work of the National Oracy Project*. London: Hodder & Stoughton.

Norman, K. and Baddeley, G. (eds) (1991) 'Assessing talk in Key Stages 1 and 2', *Occasional Papers in Oracy No. 5*. York: National Curriculum Council (NCC)/National Oracy Project (NOP).

Nutbrown, C. (1994) *Threads of Thinking: Young Children Learning and the Role of Early Education*. London: Paul Chapman Publishing.

Office for Standards in Education (OFSTED) (1995) *The OFSTED Handbook. Guidance on the Inspection of Nursery and Primary Schools*. London: HMSO.

Office for Standards in Education (OFSTED) (1999) *An Evaluation of the First Year of the NLS*. London: OFSTED.

Opie, I. and Opie, P. (1959) *The Lore and Language of Schoolchildren*. Oxford: Oxford University Press.

Papert, S. (1993) *The Children's Machine: Rethinking School in the Age of the Computer*. Hemel Hempstead: Harvester Wheatsheaf.

Phillips, T. (1988) 'On a related matter: why successful small group talk depends upon not keeping to the point', in Maclure, M. *et al.* (eds) *Oracy Matters: The Development of Talking and Learning in Education*. Milton Keynes: Open University Press.

Pozzi, S., Healy, L. and Hoyles, C. (1993) 'Learning and interaction in groups with computers: when do ability and gender matter?' *Social Development* 3(3), 233–41.

Price, S. (2001) 'Ask the children', *Practical Pre-School* 27 (updated June 2001).

Qualifications and Curriculum Authority (QCA) (1997) *Optional Assessment Units during Key Stage 2*. London: QCA.

Qualifications and Curriculum Authority (QCA) (1999) *Teaching Speaking and Listening in KS1 and 2* (Supplementary document). London: QCA.

Qualifications and Curriculum Authority (QCA) (2000) *A language in common: Assessing English as an additional language*. London: QCA.

Rosen, B. (1988) *And None of it was Nonsense*. London: Mary Glasgow Publications.

Rosen, H. (1984) *Stories and Meanings*. Sheffield: National Association for the Teaching of English (NATE).

Rosen, H. (1988) 'The irresistible genre', in Maclure, M. *et al.* (eds) *Oracy Matters: The Development of Talking and Learning in Education*. Milton Keynes: Open University Press.

Sampson, J., Grugeon, E. and Yiannaki, E. (1998) 'Learning the language of history: teaching subject specific language and concepts', in Hoodless, P. (ed.) *Language and History*. London: Routledge.

School Curriculum and Assessment Authority (SCAA) (1996a) *Teaching English as an Additional Language: A Framework for Policy*. London: SCAA.

School Curriculum and Assessment Authority (SCAA) (1996b) *Speaking and Listening: Key Stages 1 to 3, Levels 1 to 8, Exemplification of Standards*. London: SCAA.

School Curriculum and Assessment Authority (SCAA) (1997a) *Looking at Children's Learning. Desirable Outcomes for Children's Learning on Entering Compulsory Education*. London: SCAA.

School Curriculum and Assessment Authority (SCAA) (1997b) *Planning Progression in English at Key Stages 1 and 2*. London: SCAA.

School Curriculum and Assessment Authority (SCAA) (1997c) *Use of Language: A Common Approach*. Hayes: SCAA.

Scrimshaw, P. (1993) *Language, Classrooms and Computers*. London: Routledge.

Shields, M. M. (1978) 'The child as psychologist: construing the social world', in Lock, A. (ed.) *Action, Gesture, Symbol*. London: Academic Press.

Siraj-Blatchford, I. (1994) *The Early Years: Laying the Foundation for Racial Equality*. Stoke-on-Trent: Trentham Books.

Smith, C. (2001) 'Circle Time', in Goodwin, P. (ed.) *The Articulate Classroom. Talking and Learning in the Primary School*. London: David Fulton Publishers.

Smith, F. *et al.* (1991) *Looking at Language Varieties*. Cambridge: eastLINC.

Swann, J. (1992) *Girls, Boys and Language*. London: Blackwell.

Sylvester, J. (1991) *Start With a Story*. Birmingham: Development Education Centre.

Taffoni, P. and Hucker, K. (2000) 'Providing opportunities for language and literature', in *Planning Play in the Early Years*. Oxford: Heinemann.

Tizard, B. and Hughes, M. (1984) *Young Children Learning*. London: Fontana.

Wegerif, R. and Dawes, L. (1997) 'Computers and exploratory talk: an intervention study', in Wegerif, R. and Scrimshaw, P. (eds) *Computers and Talk in the Primary Classroom*. Clevedon: Multilingual Matters.

Wegerif, R. and Scrimshaw, P. (eds) (1997) *Computers and Talk in the Primary Classroom*. Clevedon: Multilingual Matters.

Wegerif, R. *et al.* (1997) 'Research Note: The Talk, Reasoning and Computers (TRAC) Project', *Journal of Computer Assisted Learning* 13(1), 68–72.

Wells, G. (1987) *The Meaning Makers: Children Learning Language and Using Language to Learn*. London: Hodder & Stoughton.

Wells, G. (1992) 'The centrality of talk in education', in Norman, K. (ed.) *Thinking Voices. The Work of the National Oracy Project*. London: Hodder & Stoughton.

Whitehead, M. (1999) *Supporting Language and Literacy Development in the Early Years*. Buckingham: Open University Press.

Wilkinson, A., Davies, A. and Berill, D. (1991) *Spoken English Illuminated*. Milton Keynes: Open University Press.

Wilkinson, A. M. (1970) 'The Concept of Oracy', *English Journal* 59, 71–7.

Wilkinson, A. M., Davies, A. and Atkinson D. (1965) 'Spoken English', in *Educational Review. Occasional Publication No. 2*. Birmingham: University of Birmingham School of Education.

Wilson, M. (1994) 'Teenagers and oral narrative', *Lore and Learning* 2.

Woods, P. (1993) *Critical Events in Teaching and Learning*. Brighton: Falmer Press.

Woods, P. and Jeffrey, R. (1996) *Teachable Moments. The Art of Teaching in Primary Schools*. Milton Keynes: Open University Press.

Wray, D. and Lewis, M. (1997) *Extending Literacy. Children Reading and Writing Non-Fiction*. London: Routledge.

Children's Literature

Aardema, V. (1985) *Bimwili and the Zimwi.* London: Macmillan Children's Books.

Agard, J. (1991) *I Din Do 'Nuttin'.* London: Little Mammoth.

Agard, J. and Nicholls, G. (1991) *No Hickory, No Dickory, No Dock.* London: Viking.

Ahlberg, A. (1997) *Burglar Bill.* London: Heinemann.

Baker, J. (1991) *Window.* London: Julia McRae Books.

Bennett, J. (ed.) (1987) *Noisy Poems.* Oxford: Oxford University Press.

Berenstein S. and J. (1975) *He Bear, She Bear.* London: Collins.

Blake, Q. and Yeomans, J. (1985) *The Wild Washerwomen.* Harmondsworth: Picture Puffin.

Blythe, G. and Sheldon, D. (1990) *The Whales' Song.* London: Hutchinson.

Bradman, T. (1998) *Adventure on Skull Island.* London: Puffin.

Browne, A. (1983) *Gorilla.* London: Julia McRae Books.

Burningham, J. (1978) *Would You Rather?* London: Jonathan Cape.

Burningham, J. (1984) *Granpa.* London: Jonathan Cape.

Burningham, J. (1986) *Where's Julius?* London: Jonathan Cape.

Carle, E. (1988) *The Mixed Up Chameleon.* London: Picture Puffin.

Causley, C. (1992) *I Saw A Jolly Hunter* and *My Mother Saw A Dancing Bear.* Collected Poems. London: Macmillan.

Cole, T. and Cressey, J. (1976) *Fourteen Rats and a Rat-Catcher.* London: A & C Black.

Dahl, R. (1970) *Fantastic Mr Fox.* Harmondsworth: Penguin Books.

Dahl, R. (1992) *The Vicar of Nibbleswicke.* Harmondsworth: Penguin Books.

Dodd, L. (1983) *Hairy Maclary from Donaldson's Dairy.* Barnstaple: Spindlewood.

Durant, A. (1996) *Mouse Party.* London: Walker Books.

Fine, A. (1990) *Bill's New Frock.* London: Mammoth.

Foreman, M. (1974) *Dinosaurs and all that Rubbish.* Harmondsworth: Puffin Books.

Gag, W. (1976) *Millions of Cats.* London: Puffin Books.

Haley, G. E. (1972) *A Story, A Story.* London: Methuen.

Hawkins, C. and J. (1989) *Mr Bear's Aeroplane.* London: Orchard.

Hawkins, C. and J. (1990) *Noah Built an Ark One Day.* London: Little Mammoth.

Hester, H. (1983) 'The six blind men and the elephant', in *Stories in the Multilingual Classroom.* London: ILEA.

Hoffman, M. and Binch, C. (1991) *Amazing Grace.* London: Frances Lincoln.

Hunt, R. (1996) *Rockpool Rap*. Oxford Reading Tree Series. Oxford: Oxford University Press.

Hutchins, P. (1968) *Rosie's Walk*. London: Bodley Head.

King-Smith, D. (1989) *George Speaks*. London: Puffin.

Lobel, A. (1971) *The Frog and Toad stories*. Tadworth: World's Work.

Lobel, A. (1976) *Owl at Home*. Tadworth: World's Work.

Mahy, M. (1972) *The Man whose Mother was a Pirate*. London: Dent.

Mahy, M. (1988) *When the King Rides By*. Bookshelf series. Cheltenham: Stanley Thornes Publishers.

Mahy, M. (1994) *The Horrendous Hullabaloo*. London: Puffin.

Ormerod, J. (1984) *Chicken Licken*. London: Walker Books.

Oxford University Press (1982) *A Packet of Poems*.

Rosen, M. (1989) *We're Going on a Bear Hunt*. London: Walker Books.

Sansom, C. (1981) 'The Song of the Train' in *Tiny Tim. Verses for Children*. Chosen by Jill Bennett. London: Heinemann.

Seuss, Dr (1966) *Fox in Socks*. London: Collins and Harvill.

Storychest Series *Smarty Pants*. Ashton: Scholastic.

Summerfield, G. (1970) *Junior Voices. Book 2*. London: Penguin Books.

Topiwalo the Hatmaker. Harmony Publishers, 14 Silverstone Way, Stanmore, Middx. HA7 4HR.

Tolstoy, A. (1972) *The Great Big Enormous Turnip*. London: Pan Books.

Umansky, K. (1991) *The Fwog Pwince*. London: Puffin.

Wagner, J. (1977) *John Brown, Rose and the Midnight Cat*. Melbourne: Kestrel.

Wells, R. (1976) *Noisy Nora*. London: Collins.

Williams, S. (1996) *Good Zap, Little Grog*. London: Walker Books.

Wilson, B. (1982) *Stanley Bagshaw and the Fourteen Foot Wheel*. London: Picture Puffin.

Index